God for
GROWN-UPS

God for GROWN-UPS

A Jewish Perspective

Simeon J. Maslin

Copyright © 2019 by Simeon J. Maslin.

Library of Congress Control Number: 2019907522
ISBN: Hardcover 978-1-7960-3995-5
       Softcover 978-1-7960-3994-8
       eBook 978-1-7960-3993-1

All rights reserved. No part of this book may be reproduced or transmitted in any form or by any means, electronic or mechanical, including photocopying, recording, or by any information storage and retrieval system, without permission in writing from the copyright owner.

Any people depicted in stock imagery provided by Getty Images are models, and such images are being used for illustrative purposes only.
Certain stock imagery © Getty Images.

Most biblical quotations are from TANAKH: the Holy Scriptures. Copyright ©1985 by the Jewish Publication Society.

Print information available on the last page.

Rev. date: 06/12/2019

To order additional copies of this book, contact:
Xlibris
1-888-795-4274
www.Xlibris.com
Orders@Xlibris.com
796103

*Dedicated to
the sacred memories
of the tragic victims
—young and old—
of guns*

CONTENTS

Introduction ix

Chapter 1: What about God? 1

Chapter 2: What about Prayer? 13

Chapter 3: What about the Bible? 21

Chapter 4: What about Us? 47

Chapter 5: What about Evil? 58

Chapter 6: What about Death? 69

Addendum: Two Timely Sermons: "Truth" and "Amos 5779" 87

    Adonai over the Mighty Waters 100

Acknowledgements 107

Index 109

Introduction

Questions

Where was God while millions of helpless women, men, and children were being reduced to smoke and ash in Poland and Germany?

Where was God when my sweet infant brother wasted away and died before his first birthday?

Where was God when a mudslide overwhelmed a Chinese village, wiping it off the map?

Where was God when a crazed gunman entered an elementary school and slaughtered an adoration of innocent children?

Where is God today as our globe warms and the oceans rise, threatening massive annihilation in the not-too-distant future?

We could go on and on with similar questions, similar outpourings of grief, similar fists shaken at heaven, similar helpless shrugs of resentful bafflement. As a rabbi, I have been asked all these questions and so many more, questioning the justice of God. Such questioning is certainly not new. The wording may differ, the catastrophes recalled and resented may be more or less earth-shattering, but the questions are all too familiar. *Why, God, why?*

What all of these questions have in common is that they fault God for not intervening, for not suspending the laws of nature, and especially for not suspending the evil inclinations of human beings in order to thwart them. What they have in common also is the notion that God is an all-seeing heavenly monitor, a superparent, with emotions that might move God to act as a benign and powerful father might act. We find a clear articulation of this notion of God as an all-powerful parent, looking down at His children from above in the book of Isaiah:

> *Look down from heaven and see from Your holy and glorious height Surely, You are our Father. Though Abraham regard us not and Israel recognize us not, You, O Lord, are our Father.* (64:15–16)

Well before the prophet anthropomorphized God as Father, we find traces of that idea in the names of a multitude of biblical characters: *Aviel* (My father is El), *Aviyah* (My father is Yah), *Eliav* (El is my father), *Yoav* (Yah is my father), and many more characterizing God as Father. The early Jewish liturgists took their cue from the Bible, addressing dozens of their prayer compositions to *Avinu she-bashamayim* (Our Father in heaven) or *Avinu Malkeinu* (Our Father, our King). Quite naturally, the early Christian liturgists followed suit, addressing God as Pater Noster. Thus ingrained in the DNA of Western civilization is the concept of God as a loving but stern father, overseeing His children from the heights of heaven.

Isn't it time finally to recognize that such notions of God are childish? Isn't it time to stop anthropomorphizing God as an all-powerful, all-knowing, ever-watchful parent, as a sort of cosmic bellhop just waiting to hear what we might want next? Surely, as the beneficiaries of a half millennium of scientific inquiry since the days of Michelangelo, it is time to progress beyond that image of God as that wondrous superhuman figure on the Sistine Chapel ceiling, floating through the skies surrounded by an entourage of angels, reaching out to touch us. I cannot say it any better or more simply than Benedict Spinoza four and a half centuries ago: "I do not assign to God human attributes." As magnificent as are the prophecies of Isaiah and the prayers of the early liturgists, isn't it time now, in the post-Maimonidean, post-Spinozistic, post-Einsteinian age, to throw off the quaint mythologies of antiquity and to conceive of God in terms worthy of the title "God"?

I love God, and it does not matter to me whether or not God returns my love.

I pray to God, and it does not matter to me whether God is moved or is even aware of my prayers.

I reverently study "the word of God," and it does not matter to me whether or not God ever spoke those words.

I listen to the voice of God even when God is silent.

I do these things in the belief that by doing them I may come closer by even an iota to an understanding of God. To approach God, we must first divest ourselves of those naïve notions of God that we were taught as children and that are still being taught in houses of worship today. What I am seeking, and hoping to share with the reader, is *a God for grown-ups*.

Chapter 1

What about God?

"In the beginning, God . . ."

From its very opening sentence, the Bible takes the existence of God for granted. Every verse and every chapter of sacred scripture rests on that opening declaration. It is as if the authors understood, long before philosophers and theologians began asserting their proofs for the existence of God, that all such arguments are ultimately meaningless.

No one, no matter how brilliant, saintly or charismatic, ever has or ever will prove the existence—or the nonexistence—of God.

If the infinite God posited by Judaism since ancient times does, in fact, exist, then that God is, by definition, beyond human comprehension. And so we shall not waste time on the futile exercise of proving the existence of God but rather take an instinctual leap of faith. We shall join the company of Abraham, Moses, the Psalmist, Job, Maimonides, and, yes, Albert Einstein, passing over the question of God's existence and asking instead the questions that have fueled the authentic religious enterprise for more than a hundred generations: what can we know of God, and what does God require of us? A religion for adults seeks to probe the meaning and purpose of life. The very same may be said of science. Both reject pious platitudes and seek truth. Einstein phrased it very neatly: "Science without religion is lame; religion without science is blind."

And again, Einstein:

> *The religious feeling of the scientist takes the form of rapturous amazement at the harmony of the natural law, which reveals an intelligence of such superiority that compared with it, all the systematic thinking and acting of human beings is an utterly insignificant reflection.*

It is not easy to talk of God and faith in the aftermath of the Holocaust. Nor is it wise to attempt to justify God to parents who have lost an innocent child. It is not only atheists who recognize that all too often, bad things happen to good people. How can God allow this? If there is a God, and if, as the person of faith so fervently believes, God is just, then how does God allow injustice and the suffering of the innocent? Don't we have the right to ask, as Elie Wiesel's fellow Auschwitz inmate asked, watching a young boy hanging and writhing on the gallows, "Where is God now?"

As an approach to an answer to these ultimate questions, I offer two hypotheticals, one in which God is seemingly absent or nonexistent and the other in which God intervenes. First hypothetical: A family of good people is picnicking on a beautiful hillside overlooking the sea. As their attention is momentarily focused elsewhere, their toddler somehow escapes from the security of his playpen and begins crawling toward a cliff. His mother spots him just as he reaches the edge. She screams as he tumbles over. The family races to the edge of the cliff and looks down at the horrible reality of an innocent little body broken on the jagged rocks one hundred feet below. They cry out in anguish, cursing God.

Second hypothetical: A family of good people is picnicking on a beautiful hillside overlooking the sea. As their attention is momentarily focused elsewhere, their toddler somehow escapes from the security of his playpen and begins crawling toward a cliff. His mother spots him just as he reaches the edge. She screams as he tumbles over. The family races to the edge of the cliff and looks down at the miraculous vision of an innocent babe nestled on a fleecy cloud, which then wafts him gently to his mother's bosom. They fall to their knees, tearfully thanking God.

Question: which of these two hypotheticals describes a God who can have meaning for us, for rational people living in the early decades of the twenty-first century? At the risk of being thought insensitive or even cruel, I must choose the God of the first hypothetical, the God who allows that innocent babe to be broken on the rocks along with the hearts of his adoring parents and grandparents.

But why? Why, in heaven's name, must we choose the God who allows an innocent child to die? Why, hearing of the starvation of hundreds of thousands of innocents in Africa, or of the young mother down the street who just succumbed to breast cancer, or of villages inundated by flood, or of the thousands of innocents whose lives were snuffed out on the morning of 9/11, or of the unparalleled evil that never leaves my consciousness, the Holocaust, why must we prefer the God who allows these catastrophes, these injustices, to happen over a God who might intervene to prevent them? Shouldn't we rather demand, along with Abraham, *"Shall not the Judge of all the earth do justice?"*

Ours is, of course, not the first generation to raise this question. The entire book of Job addresses and pursues it relentlessly. What we are doing, admittedly less poetically, is restating Job's challenge:

> *Why do the wicked live, prosper and grow wealthy? . . .*
> *Their homes are secure, without fear*
> *They do not feel the rod of God.* (Job 21:7–9)

What, indeed, do we gain by praying to a God who allows a Holocaust or the death of even one child? Why should a modern, rational person, searching for some meaning to existence, choose to believe in a God who would allow an innocent child to be dashed on the rocks? Why?

Because *if we cannot depend on the absolute immutability of the laws of nature, as established by God, then we can depend on nothing*. Either there is a law of gravity or there is not. If a baby falls a hundred feet to jagged rocks below, that baby will die. No matter how beautiful, no matter how innocent, no matter how righteous and loving the parents, that child must die. If he does not, then the law of gravity—one of the many laws of nature established by God during the process of creation—has been suspended. And if one of the basic laws that govern the operation of our universe can be suspended by God occasionally, for even the most compassionate of reasons, then we can depend on nothing. Again, Einstein: "I shall never believe that God plays dice with the world."

Just as it is impossible for the human mind to define the dimensions of infinity, it is impossible for the human mind to define the dimensions of God. We humans, in our finitude, cannot penetrate the infinite. There are realities that we accept as given although they are far beyond our comprehension. At the outset, I stated that no human being, no matter how brilliant, has ever been able or ever will be able to prove—or disprove—the existence of God. Nor will any human being ever comprehend infinity. The human mind has been able over the centuries to comprehend most of the physical properties of our habitat, Earth, and has begun to delve into the properties of the solar system. Science has even begun to gather information beyond the solar system, about our entire galaxy. But beyond our galaxy, there are other galaxies, and beyond those others and beyond them ….

Is there a limit to space? And if so, what lies beyond that limit? And beyond that? Infinity—a concept far beyond the comprehension of mere mortals. There is an incomprehensible reality that we have named Infinity. And there is an even more incomprehensible reality, far beyond human definition, that we call God. How prescient was the author of the biblical book of Kings who put these words into the mouth of King Solomon as he consecrated his newly built temple to God:

> *Will God indeed dwell on earth?*
> *Even the heavens to their uttermost reaches cannot contain You.*
> *How much less this house which I have built.* (1 Kings 8:27)

Job attempted to understand God. He was suffering grievously, and he wanted to know why. The poet offered God's nonanswer:

> *Where were you when I laid the foundation of the earth?*

Tell Me, if you know and understand. (38:4)

Can one hope ever to understand infinity... to understand God? We have only human minds and a human vocabulary. We lack the tools to comprehend eternity, infinity, God. Baruch Spinoza in the seventeenth century was not the first Jew to understand that to conceive of God as having human attributes, human limitations, human emotions would be to diminish God. As the poet of the Balaam story in the book of Numbers expressed it,

God is not capricious like man, nor a mortal who changes his mind. (23:19)

In his *Ethics*, Spinoza explained, "By God I understand a being absolutely infinite, i.e. a substance consisting of an infinity of attributes." Maimonides in the twelfth century refused to define God other than positing that God is one, incorporeal, and the creator of the universe. He rejected any definition that employed human adjectives. But we can go back even further in the Jewish quest for an understanding of God's, as it were, silence or seeming absence in instances of human tragedy. There is a marvelously poignant rabbinic elegy, originating in the ninth or tenth century, that was added to the Ashkenazic liturgy of Yom Kippur afternoon and to the Sephardic liturgy of the Ninth Day of Av. It is known both *as Eileh Ezkerah* (These I remember) or *Asarah Harugei Malkhut* (The Ten Martyrs), and it tells the story of the martyrdom of ten of the greatest Talmudic sages by the Romans. It is clearly not historic in that several of the sages mentioned lived at different times and died in ways other than as described in the elegy. And so it is not because of its historicity that we include it in this discussion but rather as an illustration of the fact that even as early as the ninth or tenth century, a Jewish poet understood that for God to interfere in the natural order because of some human injustice would be tantamount to destroying the world.

The elegy begins by describing how a Roman emperor cynically decreed that the ten greatest sages of Israel would be sentenced to death because of the sins of the ten brothers of Joseph who sold him into slavery. The brothers were never punished for their great sin, and so the ten sages, at the decree of the emperor, would die in their place. The elegy goes on to describe the torture and the horrible deaths of each of the sages, especially the martyrdom of Rabbi Ishmael, the high priest, who was beloved by all not only because of his piety and his learning but for his physical beauty as well. The daughter of the emperor, a witness to the martyrdom spectacle, seeing Rabbi Ishmael, falls in love with him and begs her father to spare him. The emperor responds by ordering that the skin be flayed from Ishmael's face. When this torture reaches the rabbi's forehead, the place for his *tefillin* (phylacteries), Rabbi Ishmael cries out bitterly. His cries reach the heavens, and the angels take up his cry, imploring God to intervene and save Ishmael. They cry to God, "Is this the reward for a life of Torah?" And a voice resounds from heaven: "If I hear another outcry, I will instantly turn the world to water. I will return the world to primal chaos. This is My decree; submit to it!"

The author of *Eileh Ezkerah*, who lived over a millennium ago, understood that for God to intervene for even the most benign of purposes would be to abrogate God's greatest gift to humanity: free will. If the Roman emperor or any other of the too numerous despots of history decides to kill, ravage, and torture, then he will do so until he is thwarted by other human beings. The ability of the human being to choose between good and evil is an essential part of God's creation. In the great creation allegory of Genesis, that moment when humanity was endowed with free will is described as Eve and Adam eating from the tree of the knowledge of good and evil. As the allegorical snake explained, *"When you eat of it, your eyes will be opened and you will be like divine beings who know good and evil"* (3:4).

The author of that amazing story in Genesis somehow intuited thousands of years ago that to be capable of good or evil is to live in an imperfect world, banished from the ease and euphoria of Eden. And that author, once he or she had described God's creative acts, also made it clear whose responsibility it is to govern the world. According to the author of Genesis, God commanded Adam: *"Be fertile and increase, fill the earth and master it"* (1:28). The Psalmist put it very nicely:

"The heavens are the realm of God, but the earth was given to humanity" (115:16). This earth is ours, to do with as we choose, to rule it wisely or wantonly, benignly, or cruelly; but whichever course we choose, God will not abrogate the gift—or curse?—of free will. And God will not abrogate the laws of nature. Natural law and human free will are essential elements of God's creation, a creation that is potentially perfect, but which can be perfected only as we come to understand—slowly, often painfully—what God intended.

Can we or anyone even attempt to define God? Our evidence for the existence of God is this universe. At some point, not just billions of years ago but an infinity of years ago, the mind (excuse the human attribution) of God inspired our universe. Was it with a "big bang"? Was it with "a still small voice"? We will never know. And so are we living in a random universe? A universe that is meaningless? No! The universe, as created by God, is the paradigm of perfection, governed by immutable laws. As we come to understand those laws, we come closer to an understanding of God.

How obscene, then, to hear God-intoxicated Jews in this modern age preaching that the Holocaust was God's punishment for the secular practices of Europe's Jews or that children in Israel were massacred by terrorists because their parents violated the Sabbath or because the *mezuzot* on their doorposts were not kosher. Yes, there are Jews in this enlightened twenty-first century, so-called pious Jews, who subscribe to such a childish and obscene theology. Albert Einstein was not a conventionally religious person, but he was driven throughout his amazingly perceptive life by the traditional Jewish search for the meaning of God. He once spoke of that search to a colleague at Berlin University: "I want to know how God created this world . . . I want to know His thoughts." Einstein's prodigious intellectual curiosity was inspired by the faith that the more we understand of the ineluctable workings of the physical universe, the more we will understand the nature of God. The religious person would add to that: and the more that we understand of God, the more we will be able to live in the image of God.

The first step, though, toward a mature understanding of the nature of God is to divest ourselves of the childish notions about God that have been promoted by religious teachers since antiquity. No, God is neither benign nor cruel.

God does not hunger for sacrificial flesh, as taught throughout the Torah.

God does not send out angels or conceive a son.

God does not take sides in wars.

God does not send rains only to the crops of those who follow God's commandments.

God does not send plagues or split seas or send fire from heaven.

God does not anxiously await our morning and evening prayers.

God is not a predictable superbeing guided by human emotions, hovering somewhere above and, like an accountant, toting up the deeds and misdeeds of human beings.

And so, the reader rightly asks, What *is* God? And the only intellectually honest answer is that God is unknowable. As we have said, the universe is the proof for the existence of a transcendent, creative intelligence that can only be intuited; the function of mature and humble religion is to carry on the search for that infinite intelligence—for God—that began thousands of years ago and that continues to our day. Moses wanted to see the presence of God; Einstein wanted to understand how God created this world. One of the great poets and liturgists of the Spanish "Golden Age," Yehudah ha-Levi, was also involved in that eternal search:

> *Yah, ana emtza-akha —Lord, where shall I find You.*
> *Hidden is Your lofty place;*
> *And where shall I not find You,*
> *Whose glory fills all space?*

Or, as a twentieth-century liturgist put it,

> *O God, how can we know you? Where can we find You?*
> *You are as close to us as breathing, yet you are farther than the farthermost star. You are as mysterious as the vast solitudes of*

night, yet as familiar to us as the light of the sun. (Louis Witt, in the *Union Prayer Book*)

Recognizing that God is "as mysterious as the vast solitudes of night," that God is transcendent and unknowable, how can we hope to approach this mystery? Can one love Infinite Intelligence in the way that the simple person of faith loves his/her God?

How to explain the transcendence of God to the humble soul who has never taken a philosophy course, who has never studied Maimonides or Spinoza, who has never dabbled in anthropology or paleontology, but who turns his heart to the God whom he adores on awaking and through every day? If my beloved *zeyde* had read all the above, how would he react? I see my *zeyde* as the humble questioner in a story by the great twentieth-century philosopher, Martin Buber. He told of an incident when he was giving a lecture on the nature of God in a *folkschule* in a German city. He philosophized at length about faith as an approach to the transcendent. After he concluded his lecture, a laborer approached him with a simple question: "In all that you said, where was the God of Abraham, Isaac, and Jacob?"

How can those of us who believe in a God of pure and distant intellect, unmoved by the daily joys and sorrows of His creatures, how can we connect with this totally nonanthropomorphized God? Ask the pious Jew how he feels, and he will answer, *Boruch HaShem*—God be blessed. Ask a pious woman about her grandchildren, and she will also answer *Boruch HaShem*. God, to them, is like an honored member of the family—present, caring, comforting, encouraging. I shall never forget the day—it was at a Sabbath service in the synagogue of my youth—when I, a neophyte collegian, walked over to a group of men who were sitting and talking together during the reading of the Torah. I haughtily told them that they should not be talking. And one of them answered, "You're telling me I can't talk in my Father's house?"

There is a magnificent example of this mindset, this confidence that God is hovering above and watching out for each of us in the classic Yiddish folksong, "A Dudele," attributed to the eighteenth-century Hassidic rabbi Levi Yitzhak of Berditchev. The Yiddish word *du* is the singular second-person pronoun, the familiar form of addressing an intimate, as *tu* in French or *du* in German. Wherever in the song translation the text reads *you*, it represents the Yiddish *du*. The title, "A Dudele," indicates that it is a little song of You.

> *Master of the Universe! Master of the Universe! Master of the Universe!*
> *I want to sing a song for You . . . You, You, You, You . . .*
> *Where can I find You? And where can I not find You?*
> *Where can I find You? And where can I not find You? You, You, You, You.*
> *Wherever I go—You! And wherever I stay—You!*
> *Just You, only You, again You, always You! You, You, You, You.*
> *Whenever something is good, You. When it's, God forbid, bad, You.*
> *You, You, You, You, You, You.*
> *East—You, West—You, South—You, North—You.*
> *You, You, You, You.*
> *In heaven—You; on earth—You, above—You, below—You.*
> *You, You, You, You.*
> *Wherever I turn, You; wherever I go, You.*
> *You, You, You!*

Is it possible to replicate this feeling of intimacy with the divine for the person who has rejected the idea of an ever-watchful, providential God in favor of the emotionless God who rules the universe with Infinite Intellect? Perhaps we can find an approach in an ancient and well-known prayer. Three times a day, pious Jews pray to "*Elohei Avraham, Elohei Yitzhak, v'Elohei Yaakov*—the God of Abraham, the God of Isaac, and the God of Jacob." Should we deem those pious praying Jews ignorant because they were taught to think of those old Bible stories about the patriarchs as fact, as history, and because they feel so close to the God whom they love that they believe that God actually listens to their prayers? No. In fact, we can take a lesson from the wording of that very ancient prayer, the *Avot*, that begins by invoking the patriarchs. In the original Hebrew, the word *Elohei*—the God of—is repeated before each of the patriarchal names. Wouldn't it have been more concise to say the word *Elohei* just once? What possible reason could there be for the repetition of that word?

What that repetition suggests to me is that the concept of God for Isaac was not identical to that concept for Abraham and that the God of Jacob was not identical to the God of Isaac. Each generation builds on the learning of the previous generation. Isaac, through the experiences of his life and the learning of his generation, had a greater understanding of God than his father, Abraham. And Jacob, through his life experience and the learning of his generation, had a greater understanding of God than his father, Isaac. It does not matter to me whether those three patriarchs ever actually lived; the Bible is not history. But the rabbis who composed the *Avot* prayer two millennia ago recognized that human knowledge increases generation after generation, that if there actually ever was a Jacob, he would have known more than his grandfather, and Moses would have known more than Jacob, and Isaiah more than Moses, and so on and on.

A tremendous amount of knowledge has accumulated over the centuries since the ancient rabbis composed the prayer book and established the rites and ceremonies that were so dear to Buber's interlocutor and to my *zeyde* and to all the previous generations of pious and learned Jews. We revere and respect them, but the knowledge—philosophical, psychological, scientific, and theological—of our century is far greater than was available to earlier generations. A mature person living in the twenty-first century cannot be satisfied with a theology that was born at about the same time as the wheel, a theology that posits miraculous revelations—to Moses and Israel at Sinai amid thunder and lightning, to Abraham on a starry night, to prophets and kings in visions. For the mature seeker, there is an alternate revelation: God is revealed to us every moment of every day in the dependable harmony of creation, the immutable laws that govern the functioning of the galaxies and the functioning of the atom.

We are the heirs of generations of searchers—Moses, Isaiah, Maimonides, Spinoza, Einstein, and so many other spiritual heroes with the courage to transcend the ideologies of the past and to probe the edges of infinity. It is our sacred duty to continue that probing and to expand by even an iota an understanding of God free from anthropomorphism and superstition. As we come just a bit closer to the edges of God's essence, perhaps we too will be able to address God as *du* and sing a sort of *dudele* to an indescribable transcendent God, to an Infinite Intelligence far beyond the comprehension—but not beyond the love—of mortals.

An obvious question: If this universe as created by God is governed by immutable laws, if God cannot be influenced by human beings, then what need have we for religion? To put it simply, why should a person who utterly rejects the idea of an imminent, providential God, why should such a person pray?

Chapter 2

What about Prayer?

If God is not imminent, not looking down at us and waiting to hear what we want, what we might even legitimately *need*, then the obvious question: Why pray? Listen to the plaint of the ancient Psalmist, impatient with the nonresponse of God:

> *O God, do not keep silence;*
> *Do not hold Your peace or be still, O God.* (Ps. 83:1)

Or the searching words of a twentieth-century Christian theologian:

> *I have always found prayer difficult. So often it feels like a*
> *fruitless game of hide and seek where we seek and God hides.*
> (L. D. Weatherhead)

How does the concept of a silent God, unmoved by prayer, differ from the atheist's contention that there is no God? Dmitri, in *The Brothers Karamazov*, famously declares, "If God does not exist, then everything is permitted." We might take the cue from Dostoevsky and declare, "If God does not respond, then everything is permitted." Why should I live in accordance with what I have been taught is a righteous life if God does not protect me from harm? Why should I pray for healing if God does not cure? Why should I care about the hungry, the homeless, and the oppressed if God does nothing about them? If God does not act in our world, then isn't all of our believing and praying absurd?

We are glibly assured that "there are no atheists in foxholes." An aviator during World War I told of how he had flown over the frontline French and German trenches on a Sunday morning and seen groups of soldiers on both sides praying. The "God believers" on one side of the battlefield were praying for victory over the "God believers" who were praying just as earnestly for victory on the other side. Surely, God must be with us because our cause is just. And of course, the same misguided faith on the other side.

And what of those millions whose faith is so strong that they reject medical wisdom and rely instead on prayer? And what of those other millions who believe that performing the prescribed rituals with regularity and piety will endear them to God while giving nary a thought to the system of ethics that was meant to be stimulated by those rituals? A scandalous example of that last-mentioned faux religiosity: just a few years ago, a pious Jew, scrupulous about every jot and tittle of ritual, was convicted of fraud and exploitation of labor in his kosher meat-packing facility. He was punctilious about his daily prayers and the *kashrut* of the meat that he sold but not at all about the basic human needs of his employees.

A Hassidic sage once taught that "those who pray for their bread will surely go hungry." By no means was that pious sage rejecting the efficacy of prayer. What he was rejecting was the simple-minded belief that prayer, in and of itself, will influence God to fulfill the desires of the person praying. Our search for an adult concept of God must not be confused by those masses of conventionally "religious" people and their priests, ministers, gurus, ayatollahs, and rabbis who believe and teach that their God is just waiting to be told what needs to be done by those who recite formulaic prayers with "faith."

And so we return to our question: Why pray? Why pray to a God who certainly does not need our prayers, who will not circumvent nature with miracles, who, according to verse after verse in the Bible, has charged *us* with the responsibility for righting the wrongs and curing the ills that we might be praying about? Why does a person who believes that God is transcendent and impervious to the whims of human beings pray? A few reasons:

We pray in order to connect with our sacred tradition, to read and speak and sing the words of ancestors who felt the presence of God and who articulated the will of God as they understood it in their generations.

We pray so that we may reverently and humbly approach an understanding of what the purpose is of our God-given lives, to help us, as Einstein put it, "draw God's lines after Him."

We pray so that we might understand our finitude and yet be inspired to recognize that very finitude as an essential element of the Infinite.

We pray so that we might quicken that bit of divinity that lies, so often dormant, within us.

We pray in the midst of a community of praying neighbors so that we may feel a kinship with people who, as we, are seeking. We gain strength from them and, in turn, we strengthen them.

We pray so that we may be reminded that God created us to perfect the world as cocreative partners.

Finally, we pray so that we may be reminded to emulate the holiness of God in our daily lives, ever sensitive to the needs of God's children. Such prayer is not intended to influence God; rather, it is intended to make *us* better women and men.

But can one truly relate to and speak to a God who is infinite and immutable? Are there such things as mystical moments for men and women who do not conceive of God as a providential presence? Yes, oh yes!

I felt the presence of God, and I spoke to God when my wife gave birth to each of our children.

I felt God's hand on mine when, in a Jerusalem mortuary, I closed my father's eyes.

I repeated the words of the patriarch Jacob, *"Surely God is in this place,"* when I sat among thousands in Jerusalem listening to Leontyne Price, with the floodlit Tower of David behind her, singing "He's Got the

Whole World in His Hands"; when I walked through the Maine woods one crisp and sunny autumn day seeking answers to unanswerable questions; when I sat on the hospital bed of a revered and beloved teacher, holding his hand in his final hour; when I stood before the Ark on Yom Kippur and joined the cantor in singing "Avinu Malkenu"; when, standing among a group of rabbis, I cried through the Kaddish on a wintry day in an Auschwitz crematorium—yes, I felt the presence of my beloved yet unknowable God at each of those times and in each of those places.

Those who pray in order to cajole God to do their bidding are like children writing letters to Santa Claus. It's cute, but it is as far from mature faith as a child's ditty is from Bach's Mass in B Minor. Real prayer, adult prayer, acknowledges the majesty of God and the responsibility which that places upon us. The liturgist Chaim Stern interpolated into one of the most ancient and well-known prayers in Jewish liturgy just this idea of our human responsibility to act in the name of God. The traditional words below are italicized; Stern's extension of those words are in Roman.

> *Atta gibbor l'olam, Adonai . . .*
> *Your might, O God, is everlasting—*
> Help *us* to use our might for good and not for evil.
>
> *You are the source of life and blessing—*
> Help *us* to choose life for ourselves and our children.
>
> *You are the support of the falling—*
> Help *us* to lift up the fallen.
>
> *You are the Author of freedom—*Help *us* to set free the captive.
>
> *You are our hope in death as in life—*
> Help *us* to keep faith with those who sleep in the dust. (*Gates of Prayer*)

Prayer, then, moves us to act as we might want God to act. Returning to the words of L. D. Weatherhead (with apologies for his male language):

> . . . . . Yet I cannot leave prayer alone for long. My need drives me to Him. And I have a feeling that He has His own reasons for hiding Himself, and that finally all my seeking will prove infinitely worthwhile. And I am not sure what I mean by "finding." Some days my very seeking seems a kind of 'finding'. And, of course, if "finding" means the end of "seeking," it were better to go on seeking.

All of our seeking—in the synagogue, in the church, in the mosque, in the woods, in the hospital chapel, in the concert hall, on the heights, or in the abyss—will prove infinitely worthwhile if we finally understand that as we pray, God is entering our hearts. As we pray, we take a small step toward understanding what God wants from us.

But—and this is a very big but—while many of the prayers in Jewish prayer books are beautiful and might move us to act beneficently in God's place, there are others that put the entire exercise of communal prayer into serious question. There is a service called *Mussaf*, added to the morning services of Sabbaths and festivals, which glorifies the sacrificial cult and prays for its restoration. A brief quote from that service is recited in all Orthodox and many Conservative congregations:

> *Tikanta Shabbat*—You instituted the Sabbath and desired its sacrifices. . . . May it be Your will, Adonai, our God, and God of our fathers, to lead us in joy to our land . . . where we will prepare for You the sacrifices that are obligatory for us, the daily sacrifices and the additional sacrifices of this Sabbath day.

The *Mussaf* service for festivals actually quotes those passages from the Torah that specify which sacrifices are to be offered on the various occasions, for example, for Passover:

> *You shall sacrifice an offering made by fire, a burnt offering to Adonai:*
> *two young bullocks and one ram, and seven he-lambs of the first year.*

I occasionally find myself on a Sabbath in a synagogue where there is a *Mussaf* service, and as the congregation recites these words, I can only wonder if the worshippers understand what they are saying. Can any civilized person pray for the reestablishment of a temple with animal sacrifices?

There are traditional prayers that refer to God as *m'hayei meitim*, the one who resurrects the dead. And then there is the twice-daily recitation, right after the *Shema*, of the paragraph from Deuteronomy (11:13–21) that promises God's blessings of seasonal rains to all who observe the commandments and *"the anger of Adonai"* and divine punishment for all who stray from God. Some of this can be excused as metaphoric language, but why should any Jewish prayer book today subject the sincere worshiper to a primitive and long-rejected theology?

Having pointed out some of the failings of the *siddur*, the traditional prayer book, which might alienate a rational Jew who has come to the synagogue to pray along with his/her community, let's look at a few examples of the opposite, passages in the *siddur* that can move the worshipper just a bit closer to God. Three of my favorite prayers may be found in the traditional daily morning service, the *Shaharit*. Believe it or not, the *siddur* actually has a prayer thanking God for the proper functioning of the digestive system. An excerpt is:

> *Praise to God who created the human being with wisdom, including in that creation a multitude of passages and orifices. It is understood that if any one of them should be opened or one of them closed, it would be impossible to exist and stand before You.*

There is an earthiness, a sort of divine carnality about this prayer, that makes me feel closer to God every time I recite it.

Another:

> *Adonai our God, make the words of Your Torah pleasant to our mouths and the mouths of all Israel, so that we and our children and all the children of our people may become familiar with You and students of Your Torah.*

What must it have done to the ethos of the Jewish people over the centuries to begin each day with a prayer for learning?

And another, this one a quotation from an early rabbinic teaching (Mishna Peah 1):

> *These are activities the reward for which are beyond measure: . . . . Honoring father and mother; deeds of lovingkindness; regular attendance at the house of learning; hospitality to wanderers; visiting the sick; dowering [needy] brides; assisting in the burial of the dead; devoted prayer; and making peace between people. And the study of Torah is equal to them all.*

I could go on to quote a dozen more prayers from the *siddur* that, I believe, move us closer to an understanding of God's design for humanity; but I will content myself with just one more, this one from the daily evening service, recited just before the *Shema*. The opening words, *Ahavat olam*, are taken from a prophesy of Jeremiah about the eternal love between God and Israel (31:3):

> *You have loved Your people Israel with an everlasting love. You taught us Torah and commandments, laws and statutes. Therefore, Adonai, our God, when we lie down and when we rise up, we will meditate on Your laws, and we will rejoice in the words of Your Torah and Your commandments forever, for they are our life and the length of our days. . . . May You never take away Your love for us.*

There is no substitute for heartfelt personal prayer, prayer that may be inspired by events in our daily lives or moments of crisis. But one becomes accustomed to the exercise of prayer through familiarity with the traditional prayers of the *siddur*. They provide us with the vocabulary and the inspiration to approach the unapproachable. We utter these prayers not to influence God but to influence ourselves to act as we believe God would want his creatures to act. A twentieth-century rabbi summed it up very nicely:

> *Prayer cannot mend a broken bridge, rebuild a ruined city, or bring water to parched fields. But prayer can mend a broken heart, lift up a discouraged soul, and strengthen a weakened will.* (Abraham Heschel)

Chapter 3

What about the Bible?

In the traditional synagogue service, the reading of the Torah is followed by this declaration, sung by the congregation:

> *V'zot ha-Torah asher sam Moshe lifnai B'nai Yisrael al pi Adonai b'yad Moshe.*

    This is the Torah that Moses set before the people of Israel as spoken by God and given to us by Moses.

    This affirmation of the divine source of scripture is echoed in most Christian churches where the reader concludes the scriptural selections of the week with the declaration "The word of the Lord," to which the congregation responds, "Thanks be to God." And the same article of faith is expressed in the Islamic tradition where quotations from the Quran are followed by the declaration "*Sadaqa Allahu al-Azim—* The great Allah is true." Clearly the three great religions that descend from Abraham all teach that their scriptures are sacred in that they are revelations from God.

    I will never forget the Sabbath service at a rabbinic convention where I was seated next to a prominent rabbi. When the Torah reading was completed, the Torah was raised, and all of us in the congregation— all but my seatmate—took up the chant quoted above: "*V'zot ha-Torah . . .* This is the Torah . . . . as spoken by God." As we were chanting that ancient formula, I heard my seatmate mumble, "Nonsense!" As soon as the service was over, I asked him about his reaction to a part of our liturgy that is in every prayer book and that has been recited by congregations of Jews, including non-Orthodox Jews, since antiquity. He replied, "We should not speak words that we do not believe. Do you believe that the Torah is the word of God? Do you believe that God spoke those words to Moses and that Moses delivered them to us? Do you really believe that?"

I answered: "You're right, I do not believe that God dictated the Torah or even the Ten Commandments to Moses, and I do not believe that the Torah is the literal word of God. But I still have no hesitation in singing out that traditional declaration of faith." As we went on to discuss my seeming inconsistency, I reminded him of the remarkable motto of the Russian symbolist poet, Vyachislav Ivanov: *"A realibus ad realora*—from the merely real to the highest reality." What Ivanov was teaching us is that there are times when we must transcend what is merely factual, reality, in order to reach a higher reality. That is the way I feel about the Bible. On the level of the concrete, the literal and historically factual, I do not believe that the Bible is the word of God. Since God, as we have learned from Maimonides and Spinoza, has no human attributes, how could God have "spoken" to Moses or Isaiah or Jeremiah or Jesus or Muhammed? And how could a transcendent, incorporeal God savor the myriad sacrifices that are ordained throughout the Torah?

Without diminishing God by the use of human adjectives, I conceive of God as the Ideal, the Ultimate, the Creative Source, far beyond human understanding. If we use human metaphors to describe our relationship with God, it is because we have no other language. *V'zot ha-Torah* is just such a metaphor. I certainly do not believe that the Torah was physically given by God to Moses, but I have no hesitation in joining the congregation in that response because I do believe that the Torah—and by extension, the entire Bible—is a search for an understanding of God's purposes for humanity. To that extent, it is divinely inspired—and I love it.

In its narrowest sense, the word *Torah* refers to the Pentateuch, the Five Books of Moses. But the word *Torah* is often used in its wider sense, referring not only to its first five books but to the entire Bible as well and, in fact, to a vast body of biblical interpretation. Since at least the first century of this era, Judaism has taught that the Torah is subject to interpretation. The early rabbis realized that there were verses in the Torah that could not be literally true, and so they established the principle of the Oral Torah (*Torah she-b'al peh*) as opposed to the Written Torah (*Torah she-bik'tav*). There have always been groups of Jews who insisted on the literal truth of every word of the Bible; there were the Sadducees in the early rabbinic period and the Karaites in the medieval period. But mainstream Judaism has always insisted that the Written Torah can only be understood through the interpretations of the early rabbis, the Oral Torah. (The classic period of rabbinic interpretation was the first six centuries of the current era in Palestine and Babylonia.)

There is a fanciful midrash (classic rabbinic homily) that illustrates the acknowledgment by the early rabbis that the Torah they were teaching and whose laws they were enforcing was far different from the Torah that, according to faith, was received and transmitted to Israel by Moses:

> *When Moses ascended on high (to receive the Torah), he found the Holy One, blessed be He, engaged in fixing coronets* [scribal ornamentations that traditionally decorate many letters in the Torah] *to the letters. Moses said: "Why do you do this?" God answered, "There will be a man at the end of many generations, Akiba ben Joseph, who will expound on each one of these squiggles a multitude of laws." Moses asked, "Lord of the universe, permit me to see him." God replied, "Turn yourself around." So Moses went and sat down behind eight rows of students (and listened to their discussion). Not able to understand the discussion, he felt miserable. But when they came to a certain subject and the disciples asked the Rabbi Akiba, "How do you know that is the law?" He answered, "That is the law that was given to Moses at Sinai."* (Tractate Menahot 29b)

What exactly were the rabbis of the Talmud attempting to convey through this clearly fantastic tale? We shall offer a few examples below of how the classical rabbis subverted the clear text of the Torah in order to respond to the realities of their day. What this story tells us is that the early rabbis knew exactly what they were doing when they tampered with "God's law." The story makes it very clear that Moses would not have recognized the very Torah that he *gave to the people of Israel, from the mouth of God* after it had been taught, however reverently, by generations of scholars who attempted to separate the eternal from the quotidian.

One more remarkable midrash from the classic rabbinic period before we go on to examine a few examples of rabbinic license with "the word of God." This midrash is a fantastic account of a debate between two of the leading scholars of early second-century Palestine. They were arguing about the ritual purity of a particular oven, as required by the purity laws of the Torah:

> *On that day Rabbi Eliezer brought forth every imaginable argument, but the other rabbis in the academy did not accept them. He said to them: "If the Halakhah* [law derived from the Torah] *is in accord with me, let that carob tree prove it." Thereupon the carob tree was uprooted one hundred cubits out of its place; others say four hundred cubits. They responded, "No proof can be adduced from a carob tree."*
>
> *Again he said to them: "If the Halakhah is in accord with me, let that stream of water prove it." Thereupon the stream of water flowed backward. They responded: "No proof can be adduced from a stream of water." Again he urged: "If the Halakhah is in accord with me, let the walls of this academy prove it." Thereupon the walls leaned at an angle as if to fall. But Rabbi Joshua rebuked them saying: "When scholars are engaged in halakhic disputations, what business have you to interfere?" Hence, out of respect for Rabbi Joshua, they did not fall, but out of respect for Rabbi Eliezer, they are still aslant.*
>
> *Again Rabbi Eliezer said: "If the Halakhah is in accord with me, let it be proved from heaven." Whereupon a heavenly*

> *voice cried out: "Why do you dispute with Rabbi Eliezer, seeing that in all matters the Halakhah is in accord with him." Rabbi Joshua rose and exclaimed: "It is not in heaven!" What did he mean by this? Rabbi Jeremiah said: "The Torah has already been given at Mount Sinai. We pay no attention to heavenly voices because You (God) have already written in the Torah at Mount Sinai, 'Follow the majority.'"* (Tractate Bava Metzia 59b)

What a revolutionary—and liberating—story! Certainly, it never happened, but why did the rabbis invent such a story? Did they expect anyone to believe it? No, they told this story to emphasize, once and for all, that the Torah must be interpreted, even liberally interpreted, if it is to survive and be venerated. If a biblical text says something that is unacceptable to the majority of thinking human beings, they have the "God-given" right to interpret or even discard it. Since the classic rabbinic period, biblical fundamentalism has been unacceptable in Judaism. There is, in fact, a quaint addendum to the above midrash:

> *Rabbi Nathan met Elijah and asked him: "What did the Holy One, blessed be He, do at that time* [the time of the above dispute]?" *Elijah replied: "He smiled and said, 'My children have defeated Me! My children have defeated Me!'"*

Clearly, the sages of the classic rabbinic period did not think that tampering with sacred texts was an affront to God. Quite the contrary, they conceived of a God who created human beings to be partners in the eternal quest to perfect the world. They certainly approached the sacred texts with reverence, but they saw it as their godly task to breathe new life into those texts, emending them when necessary so that men and women could live by them.

There are, of course, groups within Judaism today, generally labeled orthodox, who would like to see the interpretation of scripture frozen in accordance with the authoritative teachings of seventeenth- and eighteenth-century rabbis. And within Christianity, there are the Protestant Evangelicals who in their 1978 "Chicago Statement on Biblical Inerrancy" declared that the Bible "is without error of fault in all its teachings." And in 2014, in a declaration entitled *Dei Verbum*, the Vatican confirmed the Catholic belief in the inerrancy of scripture. These are throwbacks to a prescientific era when superstitious people believed childishly in angels, ghosts, and the power of the devil, beliefs fostered by a simplistic reading of the Bible, a reading which, defying the God-given gift of logic, ascribes every word of the collection of ancient texts that we call the Bible to God.

At this point, we must ask, if the Bible is indeed the word of God, why are there so many inconsistencies? Here are just a few examples:

In Genesis 2:7, we read that God created a single man from the dust of the earth. Three chapters later, we read that God created "them" male and female.

In Genesis 1:3–5, we read that God created light on the first day. Just a few verses later, we read that God created light on the fourth day.

In Exodus 6:2–3, we read that God revealed his hitherto unknown name, Yahveh, to Moses and that this new name was unknown to the Patriarchs. Yet we find that name used by the patriarchs throughout the book of Genesis.

In Exodus 20:5 and 34:7, we read that God will *"visit the guilt of the parents upon their children to the third and fourth generation."* But in Deuteronomy 24:16 and Ezekiel 18:19–20, we read exactly the opposite.

In the very same chapter of Exodus, we read that God would speak to Moses *"face to face"* (33:11). Yet a few verses later, Moses asks to see, God and God answers, *"You cannot see My face, for man may not see me and live"* (33:20).

There are numerous discrepancies with numbers in the Bible, beginning with the number of each species of animals that Noah was instructed to bring into the ark. Genesis 6:19 puts that number at two, and the following chapter puts the number at seven pairs.

Where did Aaron die? According to Numbers 34:38, it was at Mount Hor; but according to Deuteronomy 10:6, it was at Moserah.

There are, of course, excuses given for all the above quibbles; the discrepancies are sloughed off as scribal errors or are explained away by the type of sophistry that turns these texts and numerous others on their heads. After all, the Psalmist declared that *"the Torah of God is perfect"* (19:8), no errors. But any honest critical reading of the Bible must lead to the conclusion that the Bible is *not* perfect, that it is, in fact, full of contradictions and beliefs that are unacceptable to moral people today. The simple fact is that many of the dramatic stories found in the early chapters of Genesis are reworkings of ancient Fertile Crescent cosmologies, most notably the flood story, which is taken from the Babylonian Gilgamesh Epic.

If I believed that the Torah and the other nineteen books that Jews refer to as *Tanakh* were literally the word of God, I would love it less than I do. I began the study of Torah as a child, and I was taught during those formative years that the Torah was miraculously given to Moses and Israel by God. While I was certainly respectful of the Torah, the Prophets, and the Writings in those early years, I did not love them. How could I *not* respect them? I was taught verses like *"Love your neighbor as yourself," "Treat the stranger as the homeborn," "Leave the gleanings of your field for the poor," "Let justice well up as waters," "Do justice, love goodness, and walk humbly with your God."* I thought of these and scores of other exalted precepts as godly, as beautiful, and beyond the capabilities of mere mortals.

When did I begin to actually love the Bible? When I outgrew my childish awe and began to understand that these words were spoken by human beings, by men and women like me. To this very day, there are passages in the Bible, passages that I have read possibly a hundred times or more, that still move me to tears. A few examples:

The nameless prophet whom we refer to as Deutero-Isaiah saw himself as tasked by God to bring comfort to the people of Judah after the destruction of Jerusalem and the temple. The people were discouraged and heartsick; they believed that their God had deserted them. As the prophet declared, *"Zion says, 'Adonai has forsaken me; Adonai has forgotten me.'"* In response, the prophet speaks for God:

> *Can a woman forget her baby or disown the child of her womb?*
> *Though she might forget, I could never forget you.*
> *See, I have engraved you on the palms of my hands.* (Isa. 49)

I picture those pitiful survivors; I hear the reassuring words spoken by the prophet to comfort my grieving ancestors. . . . and I weep. Why? Because a flesh-and-blood human being had the sensitivity and the chutzpah to put those healing words into the mouth of God.

There is an amazing scene of reconciliation in the story of Joseph and his brothers. Joseph, now the awesome viceroy of Egypt, reveals himself to his frightened brothers, to the ten who had sold him into slavery. *"Joseph could no longer contain himself. . . . His sobs were so loud that the Egyptians could hear. . . . Joseph said to his brothers, 'I am Joseph; Is my father still alive?'"* The scene goes on as Joseph reassures his brothers that he has no intention of punishing them. What is the most poignant thing about that well-known scene? The first words that Joseph utters to his brothers after his startling revelation are, *"Is my father still alive?"* Three simple Hebrew words, *"Ha-od avi hai?,"* gasped through tears. The reader feels the anguish that had been Joseph's through the long years of alienation, decades of living as a stranger in a strange land, far from the father who had doted on him after the death of his mother, Rachel. I hear Joseph's cry—and I weep. Why? Because a mere mortal thousands of years ago understood the drama and depth of human emotion.

How does the prophet Isaiah express the reaction of God to the constant sinfulness of His people? He uses words that could be understood by any disappointed parent:

> *Children have I reared and brought up, and they have rebelled against Me.*
> *An ox knows its owner, an ass his master's crib; but Israel does not know;*
> *My people take no thought.*

This is human language, words that could be understood and painfully felt by any mother or father who has seen a son or daughter go the wrong way. And so what does the prophet prescribe as the remedy for this rebelliousness? Prayer? Sacrifices? Abject kneeling at the altar? No! A very simple prescription:

> *Put your evil doings away from My sight.*
> *Cease to do evil; learn to do good.*
> *Devote yourselves to justice; aid the wronged;*
> *uphold the rights of the orphan; defend the cause of the widow. . . .*
> *Zion shall be redeemed through justice.* (Isa. 1)

Where did a human being find the courage, the insight, the grace to utter such words and put them in the mouth of God? I am simply in awe of this ancestor of ours.

There was a very simple man, Amos, a shepherd and a tender of sycamore trees who felt impelled to speak out against the king and the High Priest because of the suffering of the common people at their hands. He saw injustice all around him while the powerful, as he saw it, "defraud the poor and rob the needy." He felt a power within himself that impelled him to expose this flagrant injustice. But what was the source of that impulse? He tried to explain it in words that could be understood by ordinary people like himself:

> *Does a lion roar in the forest when it has no prey? . . .*
> *Does a trap spring up from the ground without having caught something?*
> *When a shofar is sounded in a town, are the people not alarmed? . . .*
> *A lion has roared, who can but fear?*
> *Adonai, my God, has spoken, who can but prophesy?* (Amos 3:4–8)

If ever there were an example of simple truth confronting power, this is it. I see Amos in shepherd's homespun, uneducated, trying to make the powerful understand—to make *himself* understand—what drives him to speak out and accuse the king and his entourage. Cause and effect: God inspires, and so I have no choice but to speak out. And finally, what is his—God's—prescription to right the wrongs perpetrated against the innocent and powerless? Nothing complicated; after all, Amos was a simple man. *"Let justice well up as water and righteousness as a mighty stream"* (5:24). I read those words for possibly the thousandth time, and I am humbled. But I am also proud; these words were preserved in the Bible that *my* people gave to humanity. These words were spoken by a mortal man, expressing what he intuited as being the will of God, millennia before the Declaration of the Rights of Man.

And then there is the well-known story about Abraham and Isaac that is referred to in Jewish tradition as the *Akeidah*, the Binding. The early rabbis considered this story so important that it was assigned as the Torah reading for Rosh HaShanah in addition to its regular place in the cycle of Torah readings. I cannot think of any other story in the literature of our civilization that is so widely misunderstood. To this very day, monographs are written about the cruelty of God in commanding this sacrifice of a son, the admirable faith of Abraham in complying with this monstrous command, or alternatively, the heartlessness of Abraham for his willingness to comply. Kierkegaard wrestled with this dilemma in his *Fear and Trembling*, rejecting both Luther's admiration of Abraham's blind faith and Kant's conjecture that such a command could not have come from God. I have even heard the suggestion from colleagues that this "horrendous story" should be removed from the liturgy of Rosh HaShanah for fear of traumatizing young people. Utter nonsense!

Stories about the "founding fathers"—Abraham, Isaac, and Jacob—go back to the age of primitive storytelling around the tribal campfire. There is no historical evidence that any of these patriarchs or their wives ever actually lived, but as the saga of early Israel evolved, the stories of these supposed patriarchs and matriarchs became a sacred part of Israelite tradition. Skip over now to the seventh century BCE to the reign of King Josiah of Judah. Among the accomplishments of this reformation monarch was the destruction of the shrine in the Valley of Hinnom where people sacrificed children to the god Moloch (2 Kings 23, 10). Did this actually happen? Did Israelites, possibly under the influence of neighboring heathen tribes, actually offer children as burnt offerings to God? Yes, they did. If not, why was it necessary for the author of Leviticus to put these words in the mouth of God, *"Do not allow any of your offspring to be offered up to Moloch"* (18:21)? The clearest denunciation of this practice can be found twice in the book of Jeremiah: *"They built the shrines of Baal which are in the valley of Ben-Hinnom, where they offered up their sons and daughters to Moloch"* (32:35) and *"They have built the shrines of Tophet in the valley of Ben-Hinnom to burn their sons and daughters in fire, which I never commanded"* (7:31).

Clearly, there was an active cult of child sacrifice in Judah at the time of King Josiah, a cult that was condemned by Jeremiah and others in the name of God. That condemnation was canonized in Leviticus but even more so by the story of the *Akeidah*. Someone in the seventh century BCE, when the Torah was being organized and edited by King Josiah and his priests and set into its final form, decided that the most effective way to prove to the people that Adonai did not want Israelites to sacrifice children was to retroject that condemnation back into the story of the very first Israelite, Abraham. Abraham felt the need to sacrifice his most precious possession to God, but at the crucial moment, he heard God's angel say, *"Do not raise your hand against the boy."* And so this anonymous person in the days of King Josiah augmented the story of the very first Israelite with a clear statement from God that human sacrifice was not desired. That rejection of human sacrifice became, in Leviticus 18, a commandment of God. With this understanding of the *Akeidah* story, it too became one of my favorite biblical passages.

I could go on and on with examples of human beings who, as they studied the world around them, as a Spinoza or an Einstein studied the world around them, came just a bit closer to understanding the will of God. Scores or possibly even hundreds of men and women, living in the prescientific world of antiquity, struggled to understand the mind of God. They spoke, they sang, they wrote, they preached, they suffered—and the result was our Bible.

Before going on to share more of the beauty of this humanly conceived Bible, we should consider some of its ugliness, passages that no one with a mature theology would ascribe to God, passages that derive from human beings whose concepts of God were radically different from the concepts of the authors quoted above. Of course, we must begin with those seemingly endless chapters of the Bible that prescribe animal sacrifices.

Prescriptions for animal sacrifices make up a full 20 percent of the Pentateuch. The very same book of the Torah, Leviticus, that directs us to be holy and to love our neighbors as ourselves devotes all or parts of twenty of its twenty-seven chapters to the details of various animal and meal offerings that an Israelite was commanded to offer as expiation of sin or ritual impurity, as thanksgiving, or for a misconceived oath or for guilt. The notion that God has an appetite and looks forward to inhaling the sweet savor of animals slaughtered and roasted to appease the divine appetite is repellant not only to mature God believers today but was repellant to as seminal an authority on Jewish law as Maimonides in the twelfth century.

It is clear that Maimonides was uncomfortable with the idea that the God whom, he insisted, had no human attributes, would desire sacrifices. Yet he believed that the Torah, with all of its chapters devoted to sacrifices, was the word of God. How to reconcile these conflicting positions? He pointed out that the Israelites in the days of Moses were living among heathen tribes who practiced all kinds of abominations connected to their sacrificial cults, among them human sacrifice and fertility couplings intended to please or placate the host of gods and goddesses whom they worshiped. In order to wean the Israelites away from such practices or beliefs, God ordained a varied menu of sacrifices directed only to Himself, devoid of heathen abominations. This has become the accepted view of Orthodox Judaism. Orthodox services to this very day include prayers for the restoration of the sacrificial system, because, as they see it, each and every one of the sacrifices was ordained by God, and they are, therefore, to be observed when the Messiah restores the temple in Jerusalem.

It is amazing to me that rational people living in the twenty-first century can believe that the 20 percent of the Torah that prescribes the slaughter of animals to satisfy the appetite of God is the word of God. As early as the eighth century BCE, there were prophets who recognized that God did not desire sacrifices. Amos, for example, speaking for God:

> *I loathe, I spurn your sacrifices. I am not appeased by your solemn festivals.*
> *If you offer Me burnt offerings or meal offerings, I will not accept them.*
> *I will pay no heed to your gifts of fatlings.* (5:21–22)

Isaiah, speaking for God, several years later:

> *What need have I of all your sacrifices? I am sated with burnt offerings of rams and suet of fatlings and blood of bulls, and I have no delight in lambs and he-goats.* (1:11)

Is the ordeal of jealousy, as described in the book of Numbers, the word of God? According to the Torah, if a man suspects his wife of having had relations with another man, he is to bring her to the priest:

> *The priest shall bring her forward and have her stand before Adonai. The priest shall take the sacral water in an earthen vessel and, taking some of the earth that is on the floor of the Tabernacle, the priest shall put it into the water. . . . The priest shall bare the woman's head and place upon her hands the meal offering of remembrance which is the meal offering of jealousy. And in the priest's hand shall be the water of bitterness that induces the spell. . . . Here the priest shall administer the curse of adjuration to the woman, as the priest goes on to say to the woman, "May Adonai make you a curse and an imprecation among your people, as Adonai causes your thigh to sag and your belly to distend. May this water that induces the spell enter your body causing the belly to distend and the thigh to sag." And the woman shall say, "Amen, amen." . . . If she has defiled herself by*

breaking faith with her husband, the spell inducing water shall enter into her to bring on bitterness. (Num. 5:16–29)

Ours is not the first generation to find this primitive law unacceptable. There is a tractate of the Talmud, *Sotah,* which is based on this passage, and in that tractate we read that Rabbi Yochanan ben Zakkai, one of the greatest of the first-century Palestinian sages, abolished this ordeal of jealousy. How was it possible to actually abolish a law supposedly of God? The excuse given was that the ordeal could only be carried out in the temple, and since the temple had been destroyed by the Romans a few years earlier, the ordeal had to be abandoned. A good excuse to abolish a law that the rabbis realized could not have been of God.

Just one more example of a biblical passage that we might characterize as ungodly. The prophet Samuel informed King Saul that God had ordered him to go to war against Amalek in these terms:

Now go, attack Amalek, and smite Amalek. Spare no one, but kill alike men and women, infants and sucklings, oxen and sheep, camels and asses. (1 Sam. 15)

For whatever reasons, King Saul spared the Amalekite king and allowed his troops to keep the livestock for themselves. When Samuel came to the Israelite camp after the defeat of the Amalekites, he castigated Saul: "*Because you rejected Adonai's command, He has rejected you as king.*" Can one believe in a God who demands the slaughter of all men and women, infants and sucklings? The eminent theologian, Martin Buber, told of how this story affected him. As a young man, Buber had a crisis of faith. He had heard the reading of the above passage from the Bible, and he was distressed by it. Riding on a train, he had a chance encounter with an old Jew and told him that he was troubled by the idea that God could have commanded the slaughter of the entire people of Amalek. The old man responded in a gruff tone:

"So you do not believe it?" "No," I answered, "I do not believe it." "What do you believe, then?" I replied without reflecting, "That Samuel has misunderstood God." And again slowly but more

softly than before, "So, you do not believe that?" And I: "Yes." Then we were both silent. But now something happened. . . . "Well," said the man with a positively gentle tender clarity: "I think so too."

Buber concluded the story with these words, which sum up what should be the attitude of the mature Bible student: *"An observant Jew . . . when he has to choose between God and the Bible, chooses God"* (Buber, *Autobiographical Fragments*).

What a magnificent declaration of faith! Buber understood that those ancients who conceived, recorded, and preserved our sacred texts were human beings, mortals, who were searching for the intent of God. If they occasionally misunderstood, as we too so often do, it should not be surprising. Like Buber, people who have a mature concept of God and who love the Bible think of the Bible as a means of approaching an understanding of God. But we must read the Bible critically, with reason, always asking, does this passage bring us closer to God? And if we have to choose between a particular Bible text and God, we choose God. The fundamentalist assertion that the Bible is the infallible word of God is quite simply infantile . . . and an insult to God.

Having pointed out that there are many inconsistencies and even unreasonably cruel passages in the Bible, why do I have no trouble in venerating it and, in fact, rising in the synagogue and praising it as the word of God? Because in the footsteps of such God seekers as Isaiah, Rabbi Joshua, Maimonides, Spinoza, Einstein, and countless others since the days of Moses, I read the Bible seeking for ways to approach God. It was the author of the Moses stories who set the pattern for all future generations when he put this address to God in the mouth of Moses: *"Let me behold Your presence."* I am struck by the similarity of Moses's desire to know God more intimately and Albert Einstein's statement to a colleague: "I want to know how God created this world. . . . I want to know His thoughts." What did the author of that remarkable passage in Exodus offer as God's answer? *"I will make all My goodness pass before you. . . and the grace that I grant and the compassion that I show. But you cannot see My face, for man may not see Me and live"* (33:18–20).

Here the Bible offers us the key to approaching an understanding of God. How can we begin to comprehend what God wants of us? By emulating the goodness, the grace, and the compassion that God, as it were, revealed to Moses. But does God indeed exhibit the human attributes of goodness, grace, and compassion? This is certainly the way that most of the authors of the Bible, preeminent among them the Psalmists, envisioned God. And so we must ask, if God does not have human attributes, where did those ancient Hebrew poets get the idea of a providential God who is concerned about us and who may be approached through prayer?

There were several factors that combined to produce the biblical image of God, which has endured to our own day in Christianity and Islam as well as in Judaism. Prehistoric clans and tribes coalesced around strong leaders, leaders who functioned in the way that a father functioned within the family. Eventually, those leaders became chiefs, judges, and kings, and their leadership became hereditary. But even kings are mortal, and kings cannot control nature. And so people came to believe that there were powers beyond the control of their kings, superpowers whom they named as gods. Each of the tribes and kingdoms of the ancient Fertile Crescent developed its own pantheon and its own cosmology.

One of those tribes, a bit over three thousand years ago, began to develop the notion that there must be a primary god who rules over the others. We find early traces of that notion in such verses as:

Who is like You, Adonai, among the gods? (Exod. 15:11)

God stands in the divine council; in the midst of the gods, He judges. (Ps. 82:1)

> *Who in the heavens can equal Adonai; who can compare with Adonai among the divine beings?* (Ps. 89:7)

> *The king will do as he pleases; he will exalt and magnify himself above every god, and he will speak awful things against the god of gods.* (Dan. 11:36)

Although it cannot be proven beyond a doubt, many scholars believe that the prime statement of monotheistic belief, recited at least twice daily by observant Jews, the *Shema*, was originally a henotheistic rather than a monotheistic declaration. "*Hear, O Israel, Adonai is our God, Adonai is one*" (Deut. 6:4) may have meant, when first uttered, that Israel should worship only Adonai, *our* God, and not any of the other gods. It was only after the destruction of Jerusalem and the temple by the Babylonians (586 BCE) that we find unambiguously monotheistic statements in the Prophets and the Writings.

Clearly, ideas about the nature of God have developed and matured over the centuries since the anonymous prophet whom we call Deutero-Isaiah declared unequivocally in the name of God,

> *I am Adonai, and there is none else; beside Me there is no god...*
> *From east to west, there is none but Me.* (Isa. 45:8–9)

As we have seen above, even the greatest of the biblical authors were limited by the fact that they had only human language. They knew about fathers, tribal chiefs, and kings, and so they described God as if God were a superfather or a megaking. But they went further; they ascribed to God those features that they felt *should* characterize fathers and kings—goodness, grace, justice, and compassion. And even further, they observed the world around them and ascribed to God mastery over the forces of nature, as in Psalm 93:

> *Adonai is king. He is robed in grandeur... Your throne stands firm from of old, from eternity You have existed. The ocean sounds, Adonai, the ocean sounds its thunder, the ocean sounds*

> its pounding. Above the thunder of the mighty waters, more majestic than the breakers of the sea is Adonai, majestic on high.

Once we have accepted the fact that the Bible was not written or dictated by God, that it is not "the word of God," then what is it? Why do I, among so many others, love it and teach it? Why have sages over the past two thousand years written commentaries on virtually every verse? Why have portions of it, particularly the Psalms, been incorporated into the prayers of hundreds of generations of God seekers? Such questions really do not make much sense. Why? Because the Bible is not a single book written by one author at a particular time. It is rather a compendium of writings by a multitude of authors over a period of at least a thousand years—a period from the earliest *Homo sapiens* telling stories around their campfires to the sophistication of the authors of the books of Job and Ecclesiastes and Song of Songs as late as the fourth century BCE. Some of what those authors composed is the sheerest nonsense and self-contradictory, as we have seen above; but so much more of it is sublime, the products of human genius.

What, then, is human genius? Permit me to remind you again of the prayer that I quoted in the chapter on prayer above. It is recited twice daily by observant Jews:

> *Ata honein l'adam da'at—You favor human beings with knowledge and teach mortals understanding. Graciously favor us with knowledge, understanding and discernment from You. Blessed are You, Adonai, gracious giver of knowledge.*

Notice especially the phrase "from You" in this petition for knowledge. Ever since the allegorical story of the Garden of Eden became a part of the human intellectual heritage, people have believed that knowledge derives from God. In the very center of the garden, according to this ancient story, God planted the tree of the knowledge of good and evil. The earliest humans ate of that tree, and as a result, according to the text in Genesis, God said, *"Now the man has become like one of us, knowing good and evil"* (3:22).

The evolution of the human being that began when God inspired the universe billions of years ago included the capacity to think, to reason, to create. And so all knowledge, good and evil, derives ultimately from God. The ability to think, along with the gift of free will, has produced over the centuries saints and sinners, geniuses and dullards. In every generation since human beings emerged from their caves, there have been individuals whose intellects and abilities have by far exceeded the norm—Augustine and Maimonides, Leonardo and Michelangelo, Cervantes and Shakespeare, Bach and Mozart, Newton and Copernicus, Einstein and Freud, to mention just a few whose minds in their generations advanced human culture immeasurably. These were geniuses.

I believe that God created the capacity for genius along with the seed of knowledge planted within all human beings an infinity of time ago. While many ancient cultures produced individuals of genius—Archimedes, Homer, Socrates, Buddha, Confucius—nowhere in antiquity was there such an explosion of genius as among the Hebrews of the tenth to fourth centuries BCE. Hosea, Amos, Micah, Jeremiah, Isaiah, a score of psalmists, and the anonymous authors of the final chapters of the book of Isaiah, Job, Ruth, Ecclesiastes, Song of Songs, and many chapters of the Torah—these are works of unparalleled genius for which I give thanks every day to *"the gracious giver of knowledge."* No, I do not believe that the Bible is the word of God, but I do believe that God created *Homo sapiens* with the ability to produce those magnificent writings and that most of the authors believed, as they delivered their orations, that they were inspired by God. *"Adonai has spoken; who can but prophesy?"*

Several members of the Bible study groups that I have led over the past half century have reminded me, when I have identified a particular biblical passage as one of my favorites, that I have said that about scores of other passages. I admit it. Quite simply, I am in love with the Bible.

This is the point at which, to summarize my devotion to the Bible, I should quote all those passages that I love so dearly. But to do so would require that I transcribe here excerpts from every book of the Bible. And so I shall content myself by alluding to certain biblical themes that are quite simply amazing, considering the time when they were first uttered.

I shall never cease to be amazed by the Torah's attitude toward the stranger—the *ger*. In an era of general xenophobia, the Torah decrees equal treatment for the *ger* at least forty times. In virtually every instance where the Torah speaks about the rights of Israelites or sacred celebrations, the *ger* is specified for inclusion. In one instance, the people of Israel were told not only to extend equal treatment to the *ger* but to love him/her as well (Deut. 10:19). The reason, again stated over and over: *"Because you were strangers in the land of Egypt"* (Exod. 22:20, 23:9, et seq.). Because of that archetypal memory of slavery, the people of Israel were instructed to empathize with the *ger*: *"You shall not oppress a stranger, because you know the heart of the stranger, for you were strangers in the land of Egypt"* (Exod. 23:9). This great ethical lesson is reiterated in the lovely fable of Ruth, a poor Moabite widow, who, when she goes to glean in the fields of Boaz, is treated gently and hospitably (Ruth 2:8–9) even though the Torah rules against relations with Moabites (Deut. 23:4).

I quoted above the prophets Amos and Isaiah's disdain for animal sacrifice. The continuation of those two passages denying God's desire for sacrifice are among my favorites. What is it that God really wants of us if not sacrifices? According to Amos, *"Let justice well up as water and righteousness as a mighty stream"* (5:24). And according to Isaiah,

> *Wash yourselves clean. Put your evil doings away from My sight. Cease to do evil. Learn to do good; devote yourselves to justice; aid the wronged; uphold the rights of the orphan; defend the cause of the widow.* (1:16–17)

The consecration vision of Isaiah is staggering. I picture him as a young priest, deeply offended by the corruption and exploitation that he sees all around him. He is in the temple courtyard where the sacrifices are being offered during a sacred festival. The atmosphere is pervaded by smoke and incense and the stench of burning flesh, and he is faint. Suddenly, a vision:

> *I beheld Adonai seated on a high and lofty throne, and the skirts of His robe filled the Temple. Seraphs stood in attendance on Him. Each of them had six wings. . . . And one would call to the other: "Holy, holy, holy is Adonai of Hosts! His presence fills all the earth!" The doorposts would shake at the sound of the one who called, and the House kept filling with smoke. I cried, "Woe is me! I am lost! For I am a man of unclean lips, and I live among a people of unclean lips; yet my eyes have beheld the King, Adonai of Hosts." Then one of the seraphs flew over to me with a live coal which he had taken from the altar with a pair of tongs. He touched it to my lips and declared, "Now that this has touched your lips, your guilt shall depart and your sin be purged away." Then I heard the voice of Adonai saying: "Whom shall I send? Who will go for us?" And I said, "Here I am; send me."* (6:1–8)

What an amazing scene! It would be disingenuous to ask if it ever really happened. The young Isaiah, overwhelmed by the moral condition of the people around him and the awesome rites of the day, believed to the depths of his soul that he saw God and the seraphim and that he was chosen to bring God's word to the people. And so he proceeded to prophesy in rhetoric that became sacred writ for future generations.

Having quoted liberally from Isaiah, I cannot resist offering the reader brief passages from Jeremiah and Ezekiel who, along with Isaiah, are considered the "Major Prophets." Jeremiah lived through the trauma of the destruction of the temple and Jerusalem and the subsequent exile to Babylonia. After having chastised the people and the royal court for their sins and then seeing the horrible punishments of destruction and exile, he saw it as his task to speak words of hope and reconciliation from God. Recalling how Mother Rachel, the beloved of Jacob, died in childbirth and was buried in a place passed by her descendants of a later millennium on their way into exile, he sings tenderly:

> *A cry is heard in Ramah, wailing, bitter weeping, Rachel weeping for her children. She refuses to be comforted for her children who are gone. Thus says Adonai: "Refrain your voice from weeping, your eyes from shedding tears; for there is a reward for your labor," declares Adonai. "They shall return from the enemy's land, and there is hope for your future. Your children shall return to their country. . . . Truly, Ephraim is a dear son to Me, a darling child. Whenever I have turned against him, My thoughts would dwell on him still. That is why My heart yearns for him; I will receive him back in love." (31:15–20)*

In that passage, Jeremiah chose the name Ephraim, the grandson of Rachel, to designate the people of Israel. It seems heartless to leave the book of Jeremiah without offering any of a dozen other passages describing the eternal love—*ahavat olam*—of God for Israel. Both Jeremiah and Hosea described that love in terms of courtship and marriage.

> *I remember the devotion of your youth, your love as a bride, how you followed after Me in the desert, in a barren land. (2:1–2)*

And Hosea, a century earlier:

> *I will speak coaxingly to her and lead her through the desert and speak to her tenderly. . . . And I will espouse you forever. I will espouse you with righteousness and justice and with goodness and mercy. And I will espouse you with faithfulness. Then you shall be devoted to Adonai. (2:16–22)*

In the book of Ezekiel, again there are a multitude of unforgettable passages, beginning with the most complete and astounding description of the heavenly hosts and God to be found anywhere in the Bible, chapter 1. But I will content myself with possibly the best-known prophecy of hope and resurrection after defeat in the Bible:

> *The hand of Adonai came upon me. He took me out . . . and set me down in the valley. It was full of bones. He led me all*

around them; there were very many of them spread over the valley, and they were very dry. He said to me, "O mortal, can these bones live again?. . . . Prophesy over these bones and say to them: O dry bones, hear the word of Adonai. . . .I will cause breath to enter you and you shall live again. I will lay sinews upon you and cover you with flesh and form skin over you. And I will put breath into you, and you shall live again. And you shall know that I am Adonai." I prophesied as I had been commanded, and . . . suddenly there was a sound of rattling, and the bones came together, bone to matching bone. I looked and there were sinews on them and flesh had grown, and skin had formed over them. . . . The breath entered them, and they came to life and stood up on their feet, a vast multitude. . . . Then said Adonai God: "I am going to open your graves and lift you out of the graves, O My people, and bring you to the land of Israel. You shall know, O My people, that I am Adonai." (37:1–13)

This passage was quoted over and over again when the Nazi concentration camps were liberated and the skeletal remnants of a people were allowed to travel to the nascent country of Israel. The prophetic promise of twenty-six centuries earlier was literally resurrected in the midtwentieth century.

I could go on with scores of quotations from the Bible that move me to thank God for creating human beings with a capacity for genius, but it is not my intention to reproduce here an abridged edition of the Bible. If that were my intention, I would begin by quoting any number of verses from the book of Psalms. Virtually everyone is familiar with the 23rd Psalm, and rightly so; but what about the 8th, the 15th, the 19th, the 24th, the 27th, the 90th, and so many others of the 150 that have lifted people from despair through the centuries. Just a brief quote from the 27th that helped me personally during my thirteenth year when I was sent away from my home and family to a distant and detested boarding school:

Do not forsake me, do not abandon me, O God, my deliverer.

Though my father and mother abandon me, Adonai will take me in. (27:9–10)

And then there is the book of Proverbs with its sage instructions to children (3 et seq.) and its acrostic celebration of women (31:10–31). And of course, how can any discussion of the Bible omit a consideration of Song of Songs or Ecclesiastes? But it is my hope that our readers will be motivated to read these books themselves.

I cannot conclude this chapter on the Bible, though, without quoting liberally from the book of Job, a magnificent rebuttal of the tit for tat Deuteronomic tenet that God rewards people who do good and punishes the evildoers (Deut. 11:13–21 et seq.). Nobody knows who composed the book of Job or when, and most Bible scholars agree that there are interpolations in the text from a variety of sources. But the essence of the story is the suffering of a man, Job, who is never identified as an Israelite or any other ethnicity; he is everyman. It is likely that the primary author chose the name Job because of a verse in the book of Ezekiel (14:14) that refers to three legendary righteous men—Noah, Daniel, and Job. Job suffers the loss of his children and his wealth and then excruciating illness. He does not know why God inflicted all this misery on him. The only possible answer, if one accepts the theology of Deuteronomy, is that Job has sinned in some way. Why else would God cause this seemingly righteous man to suffer so grievously?

Job is visited by three old friends who advance their Deuteronomic understanding of God's justice, insisting that Job must have sinned, and then a fourth man joins them and reiterates their arguments. The main body of the book is a series of dialogues between Job and his friends in which Job insists that he has done no evil and that despite everything, he still believes in God: *"Though He slay me, yet will I trust in Him"* (13:15). In his epic search for an understanding of the mind of God, Job offers a magnificent paean to wisdom (28) while his friends keep insisting that Job has done some secret evil. Finally, we hear from God in two chapters that, I believe, have never been surpassed in the literature of our civilization. The chapters begin with a rebuke of Job and his interlocutors for presuming to understand God's ways: *"Who is this who darkens counsel, speaking without knowledge?"* And then the text proceeds to describe the wisdom and the might of God as immeasurably beyond human comprehension. It must be read in its entirety, but here are a few nuggets:

Where were you when I laid the earth's foundations?
Speak if you have understanding.
Do you know who fixed its dimensions or who measured it with a line?
Onto what were its bases sunk? Who set its cornerstone
When the morning stars sang together
And all the divine beings shouted for joy?. . . .

Have you penetrated the sources of the sea,
Or walked in the recesses of the deep?
Have the gates of death been disclosed to you?
Have you seen the gates of deep darkness?
Have you surveyed the expanses of the earth?
If you know of these—tell Me. . . .

Can you tie cords to Pleiades or undo the reins of Orion?
Can you lead out Mazzarot [another constellation] *in its season,*
Conduct the Bear with her sons?
Do you know the laws of heaven . . . ?

Is it by your wisdom that the hawk grows pinions,
Spreads his wings to the south?
Does the eagle soar at your command,
Building his nest high, dwelling in the rock;
Lodging upon the fastness of a jutting rock?
From there he spies out his food; from afar his eyes see it.
His young gulp blood; where the slain are, there is he. . . .

Gird your loins like a man; I will ask, and you will inform Me.
Would you impugn My justice?
Would you condemn Me so that you may be right?

> *Have you an arm like God's?*
> *Can you thunder with a voice like His?*
> (38:2–40:9)

This overwhelming poetic justification of God concludes with Job's confession:

> *I know that you can do everything,*
> *That nothing you propose is impossible for You.*
> *Who is this who obscures counsel without knowledge?*
> *Indeed, I spoke without understanding*
> *Of things beyond me, which I did not know.*
> *Hear now, and I will speak;*
> *I will ask, and You will inform me.*
> *I had heard you with my ears,*
> *But now I see you with my eyes;*
> *Therefore, I recant and relent, being but dust and ashes.* (42:2–6)

The complaint of Job has been heard in every generation since the composition of the book of Deuteronomy. All the "Whys" in the introduction to this book are aimed at the childish belief that God is sitting on His heavenly throne toting up the acts of evil and the acts of goodness of every human being and then meting out punishment or reward. The wonderful thing about the book of Job and about the entire Bible is precisely that it is a collection of assertions about the nature of God, some of which are inspired by genius and others that are flawed and primitive pieties. How can we tell the difference? Along with Martin Buber, I believe that when we read a Bible text that assaults our sensibilities as ethical, thinking human beings, we must choose God over the text. But can we ever hope to plumb the mind of God? That was the quest of Moses who asked, *"Let me behold Your presence,"* and of Einstein who said, *"I want to know His thoughts."* A true search for the mind of God must begin with the Bible, but it is not a sincere and mature search if it ends with the Bible.

Chapter 4

What about Us?

All the Western religions have codes of conduct prescribed for their adherents. And while Christianity clearly emphasizes belief over acts, the Gospels, beginning with the Sermon on the Mount, do prescribe a code of conduct that defines righteous living. But the several Christian creeds that were adopted over the centuries focus essentially on faith. The authentic Christian must believe that Jesus Christ died for the sins of humanity—*Agnus Dei qui tollis peccata mundi*—and that the path to salvation is the acceptance of that essential article of faith.

But what is a Jew supposed to believe? Is there a Jewish Creed, akin to the Apostle's Creed or the Nicene Creed in Christianity? The closest thing that Judaism offers by way of a concise creedal statement is the Maimonidean Principles of Faith, and even they, as well-known as they are, were never adopted by any authoritative Jewish body and prescribed as the essentials of Judaism.

When Moses Maimonides (twelfth century) issued his Principles (as an introduction to the tenth chapter of the Talmudic tractate *Sanhedrin*), he insisted that these principles were the essence of Jewish faith and that anyone who denied any one of them was a heretic. Yet there were revered Jewish authorities down through the centuries who refused to accept one or more of the Principles, among them such revered sages as Abraham Ibn Ezra, Nahmanides, and the Rabad of

Posquieres. Only on the rarest occasions did any authoritative Jewish body excommunicate anyone on theological grounds, Baruch Spinoza in eighteenth-century Amsterdam being a notable exception. Pharisees coexisted with Sadducees, Karaites coexisted with Rabbinites, Hassidim coexisted with Mitnagdim; they did not hesitate to issue harsh polemics against each other, but there was never a universal Jewish authority that might have banned them from the community for heresy. So absent a creed, what is a Jew supposed to believe? How is a Jew supposed to act?

The only statement of faith that might serve as the creed of the Jew, a statement that is recited regularly by Jews of every denomination, is the Shema: *"Hear, Israel, Adonai is our God, Adonai is One (or Adonai alone)."* And as we have indicated above, it is likely that the Shema was first uttered as a declaration that there was only one God for the Israelites, but that there were other gods for other people. Whether or not that is the case, what does or should the Shema mean to Jews today who do not think of God in anthropological, providential terms but rather as the infinite and immutable mind of the universe?

What the Shema means to me is that all of creation—flora and fauna, mountains and oceans, the solar system and the galaxies, and human beings—are part of a unity conceived by God an infinity of millennia ago. When the first creatures emerged from the primordial ooze, it was with the intent from God that their descendants would develop minds capable of searching for their source. Each time I utter the Shema, it is a prayer that human beings like myself may move one step closer to an understanding of God's unity and God's universe, that we may be capable of carrying forth the quests of Moses and Einstein.

And so what are we supposed to do as Jews to engage actively in this quest? And when I say "as Jews," I am not suggesting that other people of faith cannot be involved in this search for God and the meaning of life. We Jews have particular traditions that inspire *our* search, and others have their own traditions for guidance. But at this point, I must offer a caution. As universalist as I am, I am not so open-minded as to accept the religiosity of all creeds as equally involved in the search for God. Someone once said that if one is too open-minded, intelligence tends to leak out. There are religions today that actually impede the search for a meaningful concept of God. When Hassidic and other Orthodox Jews and Christian Evangelicals turn a blind eye to flagrant immorality in the highest places in order to achieve their political goals, they are denying God. When radical Islamists kill indiscriminately and destroy the art treasures of centuries, they are denying God. When superpatriots and white supremacists invoke God as their inspiration, they too are denying God and setting back the religious quest for an understanding of God's purpose for humanity. There are, unfortunately, many manifestations of religion functioning today that actually impede our search for an understanding of God. So we return to the question: What should well-meaning Jews do to continue the age-old quest for God?

Before answering that question, let me call your attention to a rather revolutionary comment in the Jerusalem Talmud (Hagigah 1:7) from one of the leading rabbis of third- and fourth-century Palestine, Rabbi Hiyya bar Abba. Commenting on the verse in Jeremiah where the prophet quotes God as lamenting, *"They have forsaken Me and not kept My Torah"* (16:7), Rabbi Hiyya takes God a step further, quoting God as saying, *"If only they would forsake Me but keep My Torah."* Now, what did Rabbi Hiyya understand about God that would have prompted him to put those amazing words into God's mouth? I believe that he was so distressed about the crude and simplistic ideas of God that were current at his time that he preferred to have people stop referencing God and rather pay attention to observing God's law.

Although this sentiment of Rabbi Hiyya's never became a guiding principle of Judaism, it is certainly a part of the historic Jewish avoidance of theology. It was as if the rabbis and sages of future generations took literally the verse in Psalms that declares, *"The heavens belong to Adonai, and the earth has been given to humanity"* (115:16). There is enough here on earth for men and women to be concerned about; we need not be concerned about "heaven." Whatever theology was taught by Jewish sages in the medieval era was in response to the unacceptable theologies of Islam and Christianity. Jewish scholars did not waste their time exhorting their people to believe this or that about God; rather they used their voices and their ink to teach God's law, how to live and act properly on earth, how to observe the acts ordained by the Torah.

Jewish tradition teaches that the people of Israel stood at Mount Sinai after their redemption from Egyptian slavery and entered there into an eternal covenant with God. The "paperwork," as it were, for that covenant was the Torah. Israel pledged to observe the laws of the Torah with the dramatic promise "*na-aseh ve'nishma* —we will do and we will obey" (Exod. 24:7); and God, in turn, pledged to watch over Israel. The book of Deuteronomy makes it very clear that the Sinai covenant was not intended to be only between God and the generation of Israel that stood at Sinai but with all future generations of Israelites as well.

> *You stand this day, all of you, before Adonai, your God, ... to enter into the covenant of Adonai, your God, ... I make this covenant with its sanctions not with you alone, but both with those who are standing with us this day before Adonai, our God and with those who are not here this day.* (29:9–14)

Whether or not there is even a trace of historic accuracy in the story of the Sinaitic covenant, the idea of a sacred covenant between God and the people of Israel, both with those who were present that day and those who were yet unborn, is—and has been for three millennia—a basic principle of Judaism. Whether or not there was ever an actual theophany at Mount Sinai, Jews have taken it as a given and celebrated it in every synagogue and school and in all the lands of the diaspora since at least the fourth century BCE. Remember Ivanov's *a realibus ad realora*—whether historically accurate or not, it has become the highest reality in Judaism. If there is any credo in Judaism, this is it: that the Jew has a relationship with God that goes back to Mount Sinai and that requires him/her to live in accordance with the Torah. Back to Rabbi Hiyya: *"If only they would forsake Me but keep My Torah."* What an amazing statement!

Let's go back for a few moments to that theophany at Sinai before we discuss the acts that the Torah prescribes for us. Here are the words which, according to the author of Exodus, God addressed to Israel:

> *If you will obey Me faithfully and keep My covenant, You shall be My treasured possession among all the peoples. Indeed, all the*

earth is Mine, but you shall be to Me a kingdom of priests and a holy people. (19:5–6)

We Jews of modernity are the descendants of those covenanted ancestors who, down through the centuries, saw themselves as "a holy people," in Hebrew *goi kadosh*. We Jews have not survived over these many centuries in order to evolve into an affluent community that reads the *New York Times*, brunches on bagels and lox, takes pride in the accomplishments of Israel, golfs in the low eighties, votes liberal, and donates over a billion dollars annually to philanthropy. While condemning none of this and, in truth, participating in much of it, I do not see any of it as providing a clue to the survival of the Jewish People. But I do find a clue—in fact, I find our entire raison d'etre—in those two little words, *goi kadosh*—a holy people.

It is, I believe, precisely because Jews have thought of themselves as a *goi kadosh* that our people has survived through centuries of triumph and tragedy, unparalleled intellectual creativity, and unspeakable physical degradation while dispersed over the face of the earth. How did those very same people who saw their temple destroyed and Jerusalem a smoldering ruin produce the Talmud and the synagogue? How could Marranos in Iberia go on teaching their children the Shema with the acrid smoke of the inquisitorial fires seeping into their secret cellar libraries? How could the Jews of the Russian Pale bury their trampled children and raped wives after bestial pogroms and then go on to inscribe Torah scrolls and found academies in their memories?

For all these Jews, the injunction *"you shall be to Me a kingdom of priests and a holy people"* was as real, as sanctifying in hellholes like Auschwitz, as when it was first uttered thousands of years ago. They saw themselves as part of a continuum of the *goi kadosh*. There! I've said it again—*goi kadosh*, a holy people. Dear reader, we are that or we are nothing! Either we accept the responsibility of living like members of the *goi kadosh*, or we must simply stop getting under foot. The world does not need Jews unless the presence of Jews inspires and catalyzes the quest for a more godly world. We no longer have accents, we don't wear strange clothes, and we can be found in every social and economic stratum of society. We have made it! And yet I hear the pitiful voice of the crazed Ophelia crying: *"Lord, we know what we are, but we know not what we may be."* What we may be: a *goi kadosh* in the twenty-first century.

At this point, you have every right to ask, "What do you mean by *kadosh*? I am an ordinary person, I run a business, I'm a lawyer, I'm an accountant, I'm a doctor, I'm a teacher, I'm a homemaker. I live a decent life. I am no less ethical than my neighbors. I am not a philanthropist, but I give as much as I can to charity. I work hard, and I am seeing to it that my children receive good educations. Why do you suddenly throw this vague theological term, *kadosh*, at me? I was born a Jew, and I shall die a Jew. Isn't that enough?"

My answer, dear reader, is no, it is not enough. To be decent and ethical, to be even the most self-sacrificing liberal, demonstrating for peace and against poverty, for clean air and against assault weapons, for farmworkers and against exploitation, it is not enough. It is not enough for the authentic Jew who, according to Abraham Heschel, "has to be exalted in order to be normal" (*The Earth Is the Lord's*). There are many decent, ethical, philanthropic people in the world—Jews and non-Jews—but there are far fewer whose daily routine is shaped by the injunction to be holy.

What does it mean to be holy? The word *kadosh* and its several derivatives play a large part in Jewish tradition. At the most sacred moment of our daily and Shabbat morning services, we sing out, "*Kadosh kadosh kadosh Adonai Tzevaot*—Holy holy holy is the Lord of Hosts." That prayer is known as *Kedushah*—Holiness. And then there is the Kiddush, the prayer of thanks that we chant over the Shabbat and festival wine. And there is the Kaddish, the prayer that we recite, often through tears, as we recall our departed loved ones. But the term, derived from *kadosh*, which I believe best indicates what it means to be a member of the *goi kadosh*, is *Kiddushin*. *Kiddushin* is the word that Judaism uses to indicate marriage. We can find in the traditional Jewish word for marriage what it means for an ordinary human being to be *kadosh*.

The Jewish concept that two people can unite in a relationship that may be designated as *Kiddushin* is a negation of the pagan view that the human being is basically an animal, that what draws two people together is animal instinct. We find that attitude in the ancient fertility cults where the gods were worshiped through orgiastic reproductive rites of total abandon. (Think of those frenzied passages in Stravinsky's *Rite of Spring*!) This pagan philosophy denies the sacredness of the human being; it makes the other into a thing, an object, an instrument for gratification rather than a creature *"in the image of God."* In Psalms, we read that the human being was created *"little lower than the angels"* (8:6). Jewish tradition places the human being somewhere between the divine and the animal, capable of participating in the holiness of God. Nowhere is this spelled out as clearly as in the nineteenth chapter of Leviticus, those compelling verses that are usually referred to as "The Holiness Code."

That chapter begins with God's riveting injunction: *"You shall be holy, for I, Adonai, your God, am holy."* The author is here making the claim that the human being can be *kadosh*, holy, just as God is *kadosh*! And then the author proceeds to define what it means for a human being to participate in the holiness of God. (Full disclosure: Four of the verses of this code refer to the offering of animal sacrifices as an element of holiness. We cannot separate these verses from the period when they were written, the period when the temple was standing and the sacrificial cult was still in force.) So how can an ordinary human being achieve divine holiness?

- Revere mother and father and observe the Sabbath.
- Reject idolatry.
- Leave the gleanings of your fields for the poor.
- Do not steal or deal deceitfully with one another.
- Do not swear falsely.
- The wages of a laborer must be paid each day.
- Do not insult the deaf or put a stumbling block before the blind.
- Be fair in judgment, favoring neither the rich nor the poor.

- Do not profit from the misfortune of your neighbor.
- Do not hate or take vengeance.
- And finally and climactically, Love your neighbor as yourself.

This formula for the holiness of the human being is punctuated seven times with the phrase "*I am Adonai,*" as if to remind the reader that these essentials of human holiness are shared by God.

There is the potential for holiness in the home and in daily life. Jewish tradition would have a family build together a *mikdash me-at*—a miniature sanctuary. What makes a home into a sanctuary? There is a mezuzah at the entrance that proclaims to all who enter that God is a partner in this home. The table is considered a *mizbeah me-at*—a miniature altar—which is approached not as an animal approaching the feeding trough to satisfy its hunger, but with reverence. The meal begins with a prayer, *Ha-motzi*, thanking God for sustenance, and this establishes an atmosphere of serenity, communion, and sensitivity around the family table. Even more so on Sabbaths and festivals, when there are candles and wine and challah with their appropriate blessings. Through these rituals, the ordinary family table is transformed into an altar and the home into a sanctuary.

At every stage of life, there are ceremonies that confirm a person's status as a member of the holy people. When we participate in a *B'rit* ceremony, when we stand under the marital *huppah*, when we affix a mezuzah to the doorpost of our home, when we participate in a Passover seder, when we listen to the reading of the Megillah on Purim, when we kindle the Chanukah lights, on these and so many other sacred occasions, we recite a blessing that includes the formula: *asher kid'shanu b'mitzvotav*—who has made us holy through the performance of mitzvot.

Now that we have introduced that word *mitzvot* (singular: *mitzvah*), certainly one of the most important words in the Jewish lexicon, we must define it in terms that have meaning for a thinking Jew today. The word literally means commandment. It is often used in a folksy way to mean a good deed, as in "It would be a *mitzvah* to visit grandma." But there is nothing folksy about the word *mitzvah* as it has been understood since the days of the Bible. The word is used over and over again in Deuteronomy and elsewhere to mean a commandment issued by God to Israel: *"I command you this day to love Adonai your God, to walk in His ways, and to keep His mitzvot"* (Deut. 30:16). And so we must ask, what is the rationale for the performance of those above-mentioned mitzvot for the Jew who does not believe that an anthropomorphic God literally commanded them?

Maimonides, in his monumental *Sefer Ha-Mitzvot* (The Book of the Commandments), enumerated and explained each of the 613 commandments, which, according to tradition, were given to the people of Israel by God. Where did that tradition of 613 come from? It is recorded in the Talmud (Makkot 23b) that a certain Rabbi Simlai (third century) came up with that number. Since there are many repetitions in the Torah and many verses that may or may not actually be commandments, it is difficult to state accurately how many distinct mitzvot there actually are in the Torah, but there are certainly over 500. The number 613 was probably derived from the ancient belief that there are 248 limbs in the human body and that each of these limbs should serve God 365 days a year. Those numbers combined total 613, 248 positive mitzvot and 365 negative.

Let's take a look at a few of the negative mitzvot that, tradition teaches us, were commanded by God:

> *A woman must not put on man's clothing.* (Deut. 22:5)

> *You shall not wear clothing combining wool and linen.* (Deut. 22:11)

> *No illegitimate child shall be admitted into the congregation of Adonai, nor any of his descendants to the tenth generation.* (Deut. 23:3)

> *Do not lie with a male as one lies with a woman.* (Lev. 18:22)

> *You shall not round off the side growth on your head.* (Lev. 19:27)

Add to these the ordeal of jealousy in Numbers 5 (see above), which describes the grisly punishment meted out to a woman suspected of adultery and, of course, the entire sacrificial system. Almost two hundred of the mitzvot identified by Maimonides have to do with sacrifices and the priesthood. These are all mitzvot from the Torah.

And so what can that Jewishly essential word *mitzvah* mean for the person who perceives God as the inspiration and creative force of the universe but not as a supernatural being who, at a certain time and place, issued commands to Moses and Israel, many of which are anomalies today? One of the leading Reform rabbis of the twentieth century put it very simply:

> *The universe is so constructed that, if I wish to survive, I must have adequate oxygen, nourishment, and exercise. God "wants" me to breathe fresh air, ingest healthful foods, and regularly move my muscles. These, therefore, are mitzvot.* (Roland Gittelsohn, *Gates of Mitzvah*, 109)

In the same way that God "wants" us to breathe and eat, God "wants" us to act in ways that will bring justice and peace to the world. God "wants" us to feed the hungry, to clothe the naked, to welcome the stranger—in short, to do all those things that generations of sages have taught us are mitzvot that we should do as partners with God in the perfecting of the world. Like Einstein who saw his role as a scientist as attempting to "draw God's lines after Him," it is the task of the mature God seeker to examine all the words that tradition teaches us were spoken by God and to distill from that mass of sacred writ those mitzvot that truly reveal the intentions of the eternal God. The nature of the world, as created by God, commands us to breathe and to eat, and it equally commands us treat the stranger as an equal, to provide for the poor, and to do justly. It does not teach us to avoid the mixture of linen and wool, to grow sidelocks, to sacrifice animals, and to discriminate against certain categories of people. As we study the vast corpus of mitzvot, we, like Martin Buber, must determine which are truly of God.

It is through the performance of those mitzvot that bring us closer to an understanding of God that we renew our status as members of the *goi kadosh*. Through the sanctification of moments and acts, through a time-hallowed process that reminds us periodically that we are not animals, that yes, as human beings we may imitate God, we are reminded that we were created *b'tzelem Elohim*, "in the image of God." When the author of that passage in the first chapter of Genesis declared that men and women were created in the divine image, the author was not dealing in hyperbole or flattery. He or she was, rather, informing us that we carry within us sparks of divinity and that like God, we too can create. But if God was the Creator, then isn't God's creation, by definition, perfect? What does God need *us* for? Yes, God's creation is perfect, *in potential!* God created a world that is *capable* of being perfect; all the ingredients for perfection are there. But what about disease and storm and earthquake and greed and hatred? Ah, that's where God's partners come in. It is our task *to perfect that world under the sovereignty of God"* (from the prayer *Aleinu*). It is our task to perform those mitzvot that move our society toward the intent of God.

One of the most familiar of the mitzvot is to thank God for our daily bread, *ha-motzi lehem min ha-aretz*. We speak those ancient words, however, while understanding full well that it requires human intervention to turn grain into something that can be eaten. The task of the human being is to recognize those elements of creation that can be utilized for the benefit of humanity. An old Jewish proverb teaches us that for every illness, God has created a cure. But it is the task of the human being to find the proper herbs or chemicals or treatments that can effect the cure. Our faith in God assures us that there is, indeed, a cure for every ill, but it is our human task—our mitzvah—to find it and thus to complete or perfect God's creation.

Chapter 5

What about Evil?

But what about the problem of evil? Why does God allow evil to flourish? How can a person still believe in God and praise God in the aftermath of the Holocaust? Why, this rabbi has been asked so painfully often, couldn't God at least have saved the innocent little children? Over one million Jewish children were the pure and innocent victims of the Nazi reign of terror, not in the barbaric past but during the enlightened twentieth century! If my grandparents had not brought my parents to the United States just three decades before the crematoria at Auschwitz and Treblinka began belching the acrid smoke that was the last trace of those millions of innocents, I would have been among them. So too many of my readers. And so *where was God?*

There is only one answer with meaning for rational people in search of a faith that might survive the challenges of contemporary reality, a faith for adults. No, God was not punishing His people (and here I have purposely used the masculine pronoun for God because people who think of God as the wrathful avenger of sin generally think of God as a stern father); and no, God was not dead or busy elsewhere. God was there, a deeply felt Presence, comforting the sufferers and mourning the horrendous folly of human beings. God was there, but *God could not put an end to the Holocaust or to any of the other obscenities of history because those unspeakable obscenities were the products of human free will.*

The greatest—and at the same time, the most terrifying—gift that God has given to every human being as a birthright is free will. We ourselves decide whether to be good or evil, and God will not take that gift away from us because it is the most essential ingredient of our humanness. *It is free will that makes us capable of our partnership with God.* Without it, we could not be creative partners with God. Without free will, we would be mere playthings, marionettes dangling from God's strings.

Ours, of course, is not the first generation to recognize that there is a conflict between the omniscience of God and the free will of the human being. If God, in God's infinitude, can foresee all, then God can foresee the choices that humans will make. Arthur Schopenhauer, the renowned 19th century German philosopher, dismissed the concept of free will with an oft-quoted aphorism: *Man can do what he wills to do, but he cannot determine what he wills.* But the essential concept of free will cannot be brushed aside with a clever aphorism. Seventeen centuries before Schopenhauer, one of the greatest Talmudic sages, Rabbi Akiba, recognized this paradox, but yet he did not hesitate to put it forth as an article of faith: *"All is foreseen* (by God), *yet free will is given"* (Mishna Avot 3:19). Paradoxical or not, this is one of the enduring principles of Judaism. God is meaningless if God is not omniscient, and the primacy of humanity in God's universe is meaningless unless each human being is endowed with free will. We must simply leave that as one of the paradoxes that Elijah, according to the mystics, will solve for us "at the end of days."

With free will, the human being is capable of choosing holiness and is capable also of choosing wickedness. Some human beings devote their lives to the alleviation of hunger, poverty, and disease, and some menace and destroy. Some seek every day to bring forth that image of God that resides in every child of God, and some spend every waking moment in the pursuit of power and glory with absolutely no regard for those who might stand innocently in their way. Some choose to respond to God's invitation to pursue the path of holiness, and some choose to be Pharaoh or Haman or Torquemada . . . or Hitler.

God would not bring an end to the Holocaust because the Holocaust was a product of the human will. Human beings *chose* to hate and envy and lust and dominate; human beings *chose* to abandon God and to deify a twisted mortal as fuhrer, leader, and the end result was the Holocaust. If God had intervened, that intervention would have required the suspension of human free will. That, in effect, would have been the end of all meaning for humanity because as we have said, free will is the essence of our humanity. God will not save us when our ill-considered acts spawn tragic consequences. For God to intervene to save us from ourselves would mean to take back from us that awesome gift that makes us human. We would then become God's puppets rather than God's partners. *Withdrawing from humanity the defining gift of free will would be the ultimate Holocaust, reducing human beings to the status of animals acting on instinct alone.*

The Torah teaches that God sets before every human being the choice between life and death, blessing and curse, and God pleads with us to *"Choose life"*! (Deut. 30:19). And if we choose evil and death? Then God can only suffer along with the innocent and comfort the mourners. If the Holocaust proved nothing else, it proved that God will not take back from humanity the gift of free will, no matter how obscene the consequences. Massive starvation in parts of Africa while grain rots in silos just hours away, terrorist outrages all over the world, nuclear madness, global warming—these are the choices of human beings.

It is not God who is today polluting our atmosphere, but it *is* God who has decreed that if the water that we drink and the air that we breathe are filled with noxious gases and bacteria, then there will be disease and plague, then young mothers and children will die of cancer. It is not God who foments crime, poverty, and greed in this incomparably wealthy nation of ours; but it *is* God who has decreed that every cause must have an effect. If a stone is thrown into a pond, there will be ripples; if a society imports slaves and proceeds to beat them and rape them and exploit them in every conceivable way and then, even after emancipation, subjects them to ceaseless indignity, then there will be urban jungles and civil unrest with innocents caught in the cross fire. It is not God who manufactures guns and makes them readily available to crazed sociopaths. It is rather those craven legislators and their deep-pocket NRA sponsors who refuse to be moved by the endless spate of senseless massacres. As one of our prophets put it, *"They who sow the wind shall reap the whirlwind"* (Hosea 8:7).

I am reminded of a cartoon that appeared several years ago in a religious publication. Two friends are seen sitting under a tree and staring off into the distance when one of them suddenly says, "I'd like to ask God why He allows poverty, famine, and injustice when He could do something about it." And his friend asks, "So what's stopping you?" And he answers, "I'm afraid God might ask me the same question." If we, having been clearly warned, go on depleting the ozone layer, polluting the atmosphere, and using our rivers as sewers, then cancers will multiply. If we, again having been clearly warned, go on exploiting masses of humanity and turning our backs on their very humanness, then there will be war and crime. If we go on spending billions and trillions on arms and luxuries and a comparative pittance on education and scientific research, then the secrets of storm systems, drought, and tectonic movement will remain hidden. *That* is *God's law, cause and effect.*

Is God, then, powerless? Unable to react to evil? Unable to cushion that hypothetical baby's fall with a convenient fleecy cloud? No, godhood subsumes all power and all wisdom, but it also subsumes the power and the wisdom of ultimate self-restraint, the understanding that any intervention that might compromise human free will would reduce us to the level of posturing pets. Having created a universe that is potentially perfect, God will not descend to human fickleness.

But you quite naturally ask, if there is, indeed, an all-powerful God; and if this God established certain laws of nature as immutable, as unchangeable *even* to save an innocent and beautiful baby, what need have we of such a God? Of what use is a God who will not save us from ourselves? Why should we gather in our churches and mosques and pagodas and synagogues to praise and worship such a God?

Ours is, of course, not the first generation to question the efficacy of God and to echo the Psalmist plaint, *"My God, my God, why have you forsaken me?"* (22:2). Twenty-six centuries ago, as Jerusalem, along with its great temple, burned to the ground and the people of Judah were led off to Babylonian exile, they quite naturally felt that they had been abandoned by God. Worse still, what if the God of Israel had been defeated or killed by the Babylonian god?

No, the silence or seeming absence of God—when the Babylonians and then the Romans burned Jerusalem, when the Inquisitorial flames and the royal edict of 1492 extinguished the Golden Age of Spanish Jewry, when bands of rapacious eleventh-century Crusaders and bloodthirsty seventeenth-century Cossacks slaughtered Jews for sport, when Russian and Polish pogromists added new and satanic meaning to Easter by decimating Jewish villages throughout the Pale, and when Hitler's Final Solution destroyed over one-third of our people, all these do not mean that God is deaf to the cries of the sufferers. God knows and God is there, suffering with the sufferers as God's own creatures murder, pillage, and rape. We are appalled, outraged, overwhelmed by despair. Some respond by cursing God, others by denying God; but still others hear the voice of that great prophet again, gently whispering in the voice of God: *"I Myself, am here to comfort you"* (Isa. 51:12).

No one who has read Elie Wiesel's first Holocaust novel, *Night*, will ever forget the passage alluded to above, the one that describes the hanging of an innocent boy by the Nazis in Auschwitz. The prisoners are forced to watch helplessly as the guards stand the undernourished boy on a chair, put a noose around his neck, and then kick the chair out from under him. The boy is so light from months of unrelieved hunger that his weight does not kill him immediately. For over an hour he struggles agonizingly between life and death. Then the narrator, forced along with the other inmates to watch this cruel obscenity, hears the man behind him ask, "Where is God now?" And he hears an inner voice answering, "Where is He? Here He is—He is hanging on this gallows."

God was there in the concentration camps, hanging on the gallows with the victims, suffocating in the gas chambers, and stealing bread for the starving. It is because God was there that some were able to survive. It is because God was there that some were able to hug and kiss their wives and husbands and children as the gas seeped in around them. It was because God was there—a palpable presence to many—that some were able to function and to face death with nobility in that time and place of ignobility. It is because the young Elie Wiesel perceived God hanging with that young boy on the gallows that he was able, after witnessing the annihilation of virtually his entire society, to question God, to accuse God, to cry with God, and yet believe in God.

As Elie Wiesel enabled us to feel, insofar as possible, the hearts of Holocaust victims, so did an earlier Jewish chronicler, Solomon Ibn Verga, reveal to us the hearts of those who suffered, as he did, from the Inquisition and the subsequent expulsion from Spain in the late fifteenth century. Ibn Verga tells about a Spanish Jew who was forced to flee with his family, whose wife was raped and killed, who was shipwrecked off the African coast with his children, who carried them on his shoulders over the endless burning desert sands, and who then watched helplessly as one and then the other died of exposure and thirst. This pitiful exile then rises from his knees, shakes his fist at Heaven, and cries out, "God, You have done everything in Your power to make me deny You, but You have failed. Even now do I believe!"

It is precisely because of the divine attribute of infinite mercy that God holds back and finds the strength to refuse to intervene and to save us from the results of human folly.

For God to intervene—to miraculously excise the cancer or calm the hurricane or provide the grain or replace the ozone or thwart the killer or in any way to compensate for the failings of humankind—would be to infantalize us, to make us puppets, dangling and dancing pathetically at the divine whim.

God gave us a marvelous and irrevocable gift, free will. Free will is the crown of our humanity, the quality that makes it possible for us to achieve holiness and to aspire for partnership with God. The Torah describes God as *"merciful, gracious and longsuffering."*

How grateful we should be for the infinite patience that enables God to see men and women, generation after generation, make error after error after error, even errors of horrendous proportion, and yet not revoke that awesome gift that defines our humanity. For God to revoke the gift of free will would be, as we have said, the ultimate Holocaust—millions of mindless and meaningless creatures prancing and posturing on their hind legs, subject to the will of a capricious Puppeteer. No, that is not my God. My God allows me to err, and if I am then wounded, my God sits with me on the low mourning stool . . . and I am comforted.

Does human free will lead always to error and tragedy? Of course not. Over the centuries, God's partners, inspired by the image of God within, have created law, music, art, healing, literature, charity, and so much else that we consider divine. Listen to a Beethoven quartet, view Michelangelo's *Pieta*, read the book of Job or Shakespeare's *King Lear*, watch a child learn, see a loved one regain health after the administration of a new wonder drug, walk through the reading room of a great university library, and realize that the God-given potential of the human being for good is infinite. Sometimes God is proud of us. Sometimes we act nobly when unbridled self-interest would have us be cruel. Sometimes we succeed in bringing to the fore that image of God with which we were endowed at Creation.

Again I return to the amazingly creative mind of Elie Wiesel and to the Holocaust. In a later novel, *The Forgotten*, Wiesel takes us to a Ukrainian village as the Germans are retreating. The hero, Elchanan, and his group of partisan fighters find a pathetic little group of Jewish boys, emaciated and ravenous, who have somehow escaped from the clutches of a particularly cruel group of German soldiers. As the boys, some near death, are devouring the food that the partisans give them, one of the partisans, Itzik, decides to do something for the boys. When they finish eating, he tells them to follow him. Wiesel continues,

> He led them to a cabin at the edge of the village where six German prisoners were being held. He turned to one of the boys, handed over his submachine gun and said gently, almost tenderly, "Fire, boy. Fire at the whole lot!"

> *The boy trembled. He looked at the weapon, examined his own hand, seemed to hold a debate with an invisible presence and finally said, "I don't know how."*
>
> *"Don't worry," Itzik said, "I'll show you." The boy lowered his eyes and said no.*
>
> *Itzik turned to another. The same answer. A third. Still the same answer.*
>
> *Itzik clapped them all on the shoulder and said, "All right, all right, I understand. Later on you'll know how."*
>
> *"God of Israel," Elchanan thought, "watch these, Your children, and be proud."*

If we have faith in God, then we know when God is proud of us, partners in divinity, and life becomes sweet. And we know also when God is not proud, when God mourns our folly. But our faith assures us that God will never withdraw from us the gift of free will. It is that sublime gift that makes us human rather than animal; it is that gift that makes us capable of creative partnership with God.

One final consideration: the question of reward and punishment. If, indeed, God is not watching us every moment of every day and toting up our good and our evil deeds, why be good? Millions of human beings go through life with nary a thought about the consequences of their acts, viewing others as objects to be exploited or shunted aside. Do those other millions who care—who provide food for the hungry, who work to preserve the environment, who abide by the mitzvot, loving their neighbors as themselves and protecting the stranger, the widow, and the orphan—act benevolently because they believe that God will reward them, if not in this life then in an afterlife? And in fact, where did that idea of reward and punishment in an afterlife, of "pearly gates" and heaven and hell, where did it come from?

There is not even a hint of reward and punishment after death in the Hebrew Bible. So where did it come from, and why is it such a fundamental part of both Christianity and Islam? We find ideas about heavenly reward in the discussions of the Palestinian rabbis beginning around the first century of this era. Why? Because life under Roman occupation was so bleak that the people could only wonder why their all-powerful God did not intervene, wipe out the Romans, and reward the faithful. One of the factors that led to the ascendancy of the Pharisees over the Sadducees—the priestly elite who accepted only the literal text of the Torah—was the Pharisaic teaching that this world of misery and suffering was only a vestibule to the *olam ha-ba*, the world to come, where the righteous would be rewarded and the evil punished. We can find a succinct statement of this new idea in a teaching of a certain first-century sage, Rabbi Jacob:

> *This world is like a vestibule to the world to come; prepare yourself in the vestibule so that you may enter into the great hall. . . . Better is one hour of repentance and good deeds in this world than an entire life in the world to come, yet better is one hour of bliss in the world to come than an entire life in this world.* (Mishnah Avot 4:21–22)

This idea of a world to come brought comfort to Jews living in misery under the heel of Rome; it restored their faith in the justice of God.

It is interesting, though, to note that this faith in a future world of reward and punishment became an essential tenet of Christianity, buttressed by the story of the resurrection of Jesus, while it became one of many debatable issues among Jews. Although Maimonides included it rather ambiguously in his Principles of Faith, elsewhere in his writings it is clear that he was referring to the immortality of the intellect and not of the body. In fact, one of the earliest postbiblical sages of Judaism taught that one should not be concerned about the rewards of righteous living, but that righteousness is its own reward:

> *Antigonos of Socho used to teach: Be not like servants who serve their master in order to receive a reward, but be like servants who serve their master without thought of a reward.* (Mishna Avot 1:3)

This same idea was taught by Rabbi Eliezer, commenting on the verse in Psalms: "*Happy is the person who reveres Adonai, who is ardently devoted to God's commandments.*" Eliezer taught,

> "*This refers to the person who is devoted to the commandments, not to their reward.*" (Talmud Avodah Zarah 19a)

Spinoza in his *Ethics* paraphrased the rabbinic teaching that the reward for a mitzvah is the mitzvah itself with this aphorism: *"Virtue, not blessedness, is the reward of virtue."* By "blessedness," Spinoza was referring to the idea of some reward from God. No, a mature Judaism for the twenty-first century does not envision a God who, as decreed in the Holy Day prayer *Unetaneh Tokef*, causes us, like sheep, to pass under the divine rod of judgment so that we might be suitably rewarded or punished—*"Who shall live and who shall die?"*—but rather a God who created a universe, which by its very nature inspires the human being to act virtuously. Again Spinoza:

> *As the love of God is man's highest happiness and blessedness, ... it follows that he alone lives by the Divine law who loves God not from fear of punishment. . . .but solely because he has knowledge of God.* (*Theologico-Political Treatise* 1670.4)

Does God "care" whether we accept the challenge of partnership with God in the task of *tikkun olam*, the perfecting of our world? Does God "care" whether we perform mitzvot? As we have indicated over and over again in this treatise, the Infinite God is far beyond the ken of mere mortals, but there is no rationale for the existence of our universe other than the belief that we and our world were created for some purpose. We were not created by God to roam the world like animals in search only for nourishment and power; we were created in order to carry out whatever we, with the help of the wisdom of the ages, might be able to accomplish to move our civilization toward justice for all. Will we accomplish this God-given task within our lifetimes?

> *Rabbi Tarfon taught: The day is short, the task is great, the workers are lazy, the reward is great, and the Master is urgent. It is not expected of you to complete the task, but you are not free to slough it off.* (Mishna Avot 2:20–21)

Is there a "reward" for joining the ranks of men and women who are dedicated to the task of *tikkun olam*? Yes, a thousand times yes! The reward is the realization that one has brought humanity one tiny step closer to a knowledge of God.

Chapter 6

What about Death?

The ultimate question, the question that no one in the thousands of years of accumulated human wisdom has been able to answer: What about death? Here is the way that a distinguished Episcopalian priest, Walter Russel Bowie, addressed it almost a century ago:

> *What sense can be made out of existence if rocks and earth and the dust beneath our feet go on enduring and human souls, which seem to be the fruition toward which all the slow forces of evolution have been working, should blindly and stupidly be brought to naught? In the face of such a universe, one might laugh with contempt before going to annihilation.*

One can hear frustration and anger in these words, and understandably so. It is the anger that was expressed so powerfully by Dylan Thomas's *"Do not go gentle into that good night . . . Rage, rage against the dying of the light."* Yes, we can rage, we can cry out in frustration, we can shake a fist at heaven, but . . . futility. We must all die, and no one has ever defeated death. And so let's start there, with those stories about characters who are *supposed* to have defeated or returned from death.

Among the Babylonians, as recounted in the Gilgamesh Epic, it was the god Tammuz who was brought back to life by Ishtar. The Egyptians told of Osiris who was resurrected by Isis. For the Greeks, it was Persephone, carried away to the netherworld by Hades and resurrected each spring through the tears of her mother, Demeter. The Norse told about Baldur and the Aztecs about Quetzalcoatl. According to Carl Jung, these ubiquitous myths of resurrected pagan gods foreshadowed the story that lies at the heart of Christianity, the resurrection of Jesus.

While the Christian resurrection story, celebrated for almost two millennia each year on Easter when churches display banners proclaiming "He is risen" was certainly influenced by pagan mythology, there was also considerable support in the teachings of the first- and second-century rabbis. They may have rejected the claim that a particular itinerant preacher from Galilee did actually rise from the dead, but they injected into Judaism the idea that death is a temporary state and that God will bring the dead back to life. These early rabbis established the belief in *t'hiat ha-metim* (restoring the dead to life, i.e., resurrection) as one of the central doctrines of Judaism:

> *All of Israel has a portion in the world to come, as it is said: (*Isa. 60:2) *"And Thy people are all righteous; at the End they shall inherit the land. . . ." But the following have no portion in the world to come; one who says that there is no resurrection of the dead and one who denies the divine authorship of the Torah.* (Mishna Sanhedrin 10)

So essential was this belief in bodily resurrection to the early rabbis that they equated it with the axiomatic belief that God was the source of the Torah, and they included it in the liturgy that they prescribed for daily worship, especially in the second of the eighteen benedictions of the Amidah:

> *You sustain the living with lovingkindness, revive the dead with great mercy, . . . and keep faith with those who sleep in the dust. . . . You are faithful in granting eternal life to the dead. Blessed are You who resurrects the dead.* (every traditional Jewish prayer book)

There were those who disagreed with the early rabbis, most notably the Sadducees who would not accept any tenet that wasn't stated specifically in the Bible, but there were also sociological reasons for their denial of resurrection. Most of the early rabbis came from the ranks of ordinary people; they had to work for their living, and they were victims, as were all ordinary Judaeans during the first three centuries of the Common Era, of the cruel, often murderous regime of the Romans. They were, for the most part, the Pharisees. The Sadducees, on the other hand, were the priestly class and the gentry, often working hand-in-hand with the Romans. They were not subject to the same sufferings that typified the lives of ordinary Judeans.

One can readily understand why a second-century Jew might ask one of the learned rabbis why they should observe the myriad of mitzvot ordained by the Torah if their Jewish observances subjected them to the cruel lash of the Romans. And so was born the concept of *t'hiat ha-metim*. You may be suffering in this world, the rabbi would reply, but that suffering will be rewarded in the next world, in the *Olam Ha-emet*, the real world. One of those second-century sages, Rabbi Jacob, representing the Pharisaic belief, put it quite succinctly:

> *This world is like a foyer leading to the world to come. Prepare yourself in the foyer so that you may be allowed to enter the great hall.* (Mishna Avot 4:21)

Rabbi Jacob continued his lesson by referring to the period after death as "*blissfulness of spirit in the world to come.*"

Now those rabbis would not have had the temerity to invent the idea of life after death out of whole cloth; they needed some biblical underpinning. But while there is certainly no clearly spelled-out doctrine of resurrection anywhere in the Bible, there are several verses that might be taken to support the idea. A few examples:

> *Adonai kills and gives life; brings down to Sheol and brings up.* (1 Sam. 2:6)

> *Adonai, You have brought me up from Sheol.* (Ps. 30:4)

> *Many of them that sleep in the dust of the earth shall awake, some to everlasting life and some to reproaches.* (Dan. 12:2)

But overwhelmingly, the biblical authors saw death as the absolute end of life. The poignant lament of Job is an accurate representation of the biblical view of death:

> *Remember, my life is but a breath of wind; I shall never again see good days.*
>
> *You will behold me no more; under your very eyes, I shall disappear. As clouds break up and disperse, so one who goes down to Sheol never comes back; he never returns home again, and his place will know him no more.* (Job 7:7–9)

Shakespeare put what should be the final word on the subject into Hamlet's soliloquy:

> *Death, the undiscovered country from whose bourn no traveler returns.* (3:47)

But of course, that is not the final word. A major part of religious faith—Jewish, Christian, and Islamic—since the days of the early rabbis has concerned itself with what happens to a person after death. I am not referring here to the question of resurrection, actually emerging from the grave and resuming animated life. What I am referring to is the belief that after death, the person is transported to a place of purgation and/or reward. That belief, in its various forms, is common to all three of the Western religions and is derived from early mythologies. In the Babylonian *Gilgamesh Epic*, the netherworld is depicted as

> *the land of no return . . . the dark house . . . the house which none leave . . . the house in which the entrants are deprived of light, where dust is their fare and clay their food, where they see no light, residing in darkness.*

And there are similar descriptions of the place to which the dead are consigned in virtually all the early Western mythologies.

Jewish tradition, since the period of the early rabbis—first and second centuries—has taught that the dead are judged by a heavenly tribunal and are consigned either to *Gan Eden* (Paradise, literally "the garden of Eden") or to *Gehinnom* (*Gehinnom* is derived from *Gai Hinnom*, the Valley of Hinnom where the rite of child sacrifice through fire was practiced in the sixth and seventh centuries BCE). That tradition, with numerous citations in the Talmud, the Midrash, and especially in medieval folklore, is replete with graphic descriptions of the sufferings of sinners after death.

In the tractate *Rosh HaShanah* of the Babylonian Talmud, there are two passages that describe the early Pharisaic understanding of what happens after death:

> *Sinners of Israel who sin with their bodies and sinners of the Gentiles who sin with their bodies go down to Gehinnom and are punished there for twelve months. After twelve months their bodies are consumed and their souls are burnt and the wind scatters them under the soles of the righteous, as it says. (Mal. 3:2) "And you shall tread down the wicked, and they shall be as ashes under the soles of your feet." For those . . . who rejected the Torah and denied the resurrection of the dead . . . and sinned and made the masses sin . . ., they will go down to Gehinnom and be punished there for all generations, as it says. (Isa. 66:24) "They shall go forth and gaze at the corpses of the men who have rebelled against Me. Their worms shall not die nor their fire be quenched; they shall be a horror to all flesh."* (Rosh HaShanah 17a)

> *"The School of Shammai taught: There will be three groups at the Day of Judgment—one of the thoroughly righteous, one of the thoroughly wicked, and one of the intermediate. The thoroughly righteous will be definitely inscribed as entitled to everlasting life; the thoroughly wicked will be definitely inscribed as doomed to Gehinnom. . . . The intermediates will go down to Gehinnom and shriek and rise again, as it says. (Zech. 13:9) "I will bring*

> *the third part through the fire and will refine them as silver is refined."* (Rosh HaShanah 16b)

As indicated in the former passage, purgation in Gehinnom was thought to last for only twelve months. Rabbi Akiba taught,

> *The punishment for the [wicked] generation of the flood was twelve months;*
> *the punishment for Job [who questioned God] was for twelve months;*
> *the punishment for the Egyptians was twelve months;*
> *the punishment for Gog and Magog (kings who will fight against Israel at the end of time) will be for twelve months;*
> *the punishment for sinners in Gehinnom will be for twelve months.* (Mishnah Eduyot 2:10)

Rabbi Akiba went on to offer a rather far-fetched biblical source for the belief that all who have sinned during their lifetimes will suffer purgation for twelve months, but far-fetched or not, this teaching by one of the most eminent second-century sages has persisted in Judaism to our very day. It explains why the children of deceased parents recite the Kaddish (the prayer for the souls of the dead; see below) for eleven months. For if they were to recite it for a full twelve months, they would be indicating that their parents were so wicked that they deserved the full twelve-month purgation. If this sounds silly to the modern ear, you're right, it is!

The preeminent Jewish philosopher of the Middle Ages, the rationalist Moses Maimonides, was clearly embarrassed by the graphic descriptions of the fleshly torments of Gehinnom, but there was no way he could deny what the authoritative sages of the Mishnah had posited as a fundamental principle of Judaism. And so he incorporated the belief in reward and punishment and the belief in the revival of the dead as the eleventh and final of his "Thirteen Principles of Faith." But he made it very clear elsewhere that it was the souls and not the bodies of the dead that were punished or rewarded.

What does—or did—Christianity teach about the fate of the dead? One of the best-known of those teachings may be found in the Gospel of Mark. (It should be noted that most Christian Bible translations use the word *Hell* as the translation for Gehinnom.)

> *If your hand is your undoing, cut it off; it is better for you to enter into life maimed than to keep both hands and go to hell and the unquenchable fire. And if your foot is your undoing, cut if off; it is better to enter into life a cripple than to keep both your feet and be thrown into hell. And if it is your eye, tear it out; it is better to enter into the kingdom of God with one eye than to keep both eyes and be thrown into hell; where the devouring worm never dies and the fire is not quenched.* (Mark 9:43–48)

Granted that Mark (as well as a similar passage in Matthew) was employing hyperbole to make his point, but his point was that sinners are punished with the torments of Hell (or Gehinnom), which is exactly what the Pharisaic sages were teaching at the time. (How ironic that the Christian Bible, which so often condemns the Pharisees, is full of Pharisaic teachings!)

Just two more New Testament texts on postmortem purgation:

> *Do not fear those who kill the body but cannot kill the soul. Fear him rather who is able to destroy both soul and body in Hell.* (Matt. 10:28 and Luke 12:4–5)

> *The rich man also died and was buried, and in Hades, where he was in torment, he looked up; and there, far away, was Abraham with Lazarus close beside him. "Abraham, my father," he called out, "take pity on me! Send Lazarus to dip the tip of his finger in water, to cool my tongue, for I am in agony in this fire."* (Luke 16:22–24)

This last text goes on to explain that Abraham and Lazarus could not help the rich man in Hades because *"there is a great chasm fixed between us; no one . . . can cross it."* Here we have the foreshadowing of the geography of Hell that was detailed centuries later by Dante.

About half a millennium after the writings of the early rabbis and the Gospel writers on the punishments that await the sinner after death, Islam was born and incorporated that article of faith into the Quran. The place of punishment in the Quran is called Jahannam, obviously derived from the Gehinnom of early Jewish and Christian texts. References to the punishments that sinners will suffer are found throughout the Quran. This one is clearly derived from the Luke passage above:

> *And the companions of the Fire [al-nar] will call to the companions of Paradise, "Pour upon us some water or from whatever Allah has provided you," They will, say, "Indeed, Allah has forbidden them both to the disbelievers."* (Quran 17:50)

The Quran speaks of the seven levels of Jahannam and gives names to its different gates, again anticipating Dante's topography. And so now we skip ahead about six centuries to Dante.

Inspired by the writings of Thomas Aquinas, Dante Alighieri, a fourteenth-century Italian, composed what is widely considered to be the greatest work of Italian literature, *The Divine Comedy*. In magnificent poetry, Dante described his travels through the several levels of the abode of the dead, the Inferno, Purgatory, and Paradise. He is guided through the netherworld by Virgil and through Paradise by his beloved Beatrice. He describes in detail the punishments suffered by various groups of sinners in the Inferno, for example, gluttons are forced to lie in vile slush, heretics lie in fiery tombs, the treacherous are frozen in an icy lake, fortunetellers walk around with their heads on backward for falsely predicting the future, and so on.

What is the point of all the above recounting of the systems of reward and punishment in the afterlife as described in pagan mythology, in the writings of the early rabbis, the Gospels, and the Quran? The point is that all those descriptions stem from early mythology and were later incorporated into the canons of the Western religions. No one, ancient or modern, knows anything about what happens to the body or the soul of the deceased. There is a common psychological need to believe in ultimate justice. Evil *must* be punished, and righteousness *must* be rewarded. But the astute observer knows from everything that he/she sees in life that this is not always the case. Ah, but it *must* be true, and so we return to the Mishnah Avot: *"This life is like a foyer leading into the world to come."* The only way the ancient mind could justify the disparity between the powerful and the meek, between the sinners and the righteous, was to envision what the early rabbis called the *Olam ha-Emet*, the real world, that is, a place of reward and punishment after death. But . . .

The fact that this other world is described in detail in some of the most beautiful poetic imagery conceived by the human mind does not make it true. Rabbis, priests, imams, and other religious functionaries have been preaching about reward and punishment after death, about hell and paradise, for centuries. Waving their Bibles or Qurans and shouting their warnings with the deepest conviction and certainty, they have successfully planted this article of faith into the psyches of billions of people. The pearly gates, the forty virgins waiting for jihadists, the devil and angels with fleecy wings—all these images have been sold as truths for centuries. They are as much a part of the human consciousness as a toothache. What is actually the truth? The truth is that we know nothing about what may or may not happen after death. We know nothing, absolutely nothing, about *"the undiscovered country from whose bourn no traveler returns."*

But is there anything that we *do* know? Yes, we know what modern science has proven beyond a doubt, and that is that our DNA is immortal. There are traces of our ancient forebears in every one of us, and not only in our physiognomies. The stamp of our parents and their parents are evident in our intellect, in our attitudes, in our likes and dislikes, and, for better or for worse, in everything that we are and that we do. That is not to say that our lives are predetermined by our genes. Here we get back to free choice, as discussed above. Every human being is endowed with the genetic material of previous generations, but every human being is also endowed with the ability to choose.

There is an essential teaching in the Passover ritual, the Haggadah, that goes back to the earliest rabbis. At the climactic moment of the service, before the traditional meal, the text reads, *"In every generation a* person is required to think of him/herself as if personally freed from Egypt." The idea that we, living today, were there with the generation of Moses and the freed slaves is reiterated in the book of Deuteronomy where Moses addressed not only those of his generation *"but also with those who are not with us this day"* (29:14). Through the genes that we inherited, *we* were slaves in Egypt, *we* stood at Sinai, *we* sat in the academies of Hillel and Akiba. All of this is in our DNA; we are immortal.

We opened this discussion of death by quoting a few lines from a meditation by the Episcopalian priest, Walter Russel Bowie. Bowie spoke of rocks and dust enduring eternally while human beings are stupidly "brought to naught." Faced with this reality, one *"might laugh with contempt before he went to his annihilation."* Then Bowie continues,

> But we cannot believe that contemptuous laughter is the ultimate verdict to be passed upon our world. There must be in it something that has caused our own ideals, something akin to our passion for continuing life, and something upon which we can rely. God must be in it, and God is life, and God is love. Even in the moments when our intellect is baffled, and even in those times when contradictions beset our faith, still we refuse to be put to permanent intellectual and spiritual confusion, and still our deepest souls declare that beyond the shadows there is light, and in the depths of the utmost darkness life goes upon its undefeated way.

"God must be in it," here we return to our first consideration: What about God? How is God, the Infinite Intelligence who transcends the daily affairs of human beings, involved in the deaths of our mothers and fathers, our husbands and wives, our loved ones and the homeless derelict sleeping on the sidewalk? How is God involved in our own deaths?

When the mind of God created our world and the organisms that would evolve into *Homo sapiens* billions of years ago, that infinite mind created genetic codes that would evolve along with their carriers, and that would survive through all the generations from the primordial ooze to you and me today. Our ideals, our intellect, and our passions were latent in the earliest organism that emerged from that ooze. That evolutionary spiral was designed by God, the God who is the source of life, the God who is infinitely beyond human understanding, the God whose love makes it possible for us to continue the search of Moses and Spinoza and Einstein. That is our immortality, not a netherworld barbecue and not a heavenly fairyland, but the innate assurance that the evolutionary process is eternal and that a part of us will one day explore the far reaches of infinity.

We mentioned above the recitation of the Kaddish prayer in memory of our dead and the rather ridiculous custom that the mourners should recite it for only eleven months so as not to imply that their loved ones are sentenced to the full twelve months in Gehinnom. But if we do not accept the childish notion of physical reward and punishment after death, why recite the Kaddish at all? What does it have to do with death and mourning? The answer is that there is absolutely nothing about death in the Kaddish. That prayer is a doxology, a paean of praise to God, written in the Aramaic that scholars spoke in the academies of first-century Jerusalem.

So how did the custom develop to recite the Kaddish as a prayer for the dead? It was the practice of those scholars to conclude the study of sacred scriptures with a prayer of thanks to God for the privilege of learning. The teacher would dismiss his class with words inspired by the messianic verse in the book of Ezekiel: *"Thus will I manifest My greatness and My holiness . . . in the sight of many nations."* He would say, *"Yitgadal ve-yitkadash shemei Rabbah*—May the greatness and the holiness of God's name be manifest," continuing in that mode of praise, to which the students would respond, *"Amen! May His great name be blessed forever and ever."*

At some point, scholars would begin reciting this familiar doxology at the funerals of learned rabbis, the idea being that their deaths were like the conclusion of the study of a sacred text. This custom became rather widespread so that many considered it to be a slight if these words were not recited at a person's funeral. Then in medieval times, there developed a popular legend that Rabbi Akiba saved a tortured soul from the tortures of Gehinnom by teaching his son to recite the Kaddish. That did it. Since early medieval times, Jews have recited the Kaddish at funerals even though the text has not one word about death.

Here is the original text of the Kaddish:

> *May the greatness and the holiness of God's name be manifest in the world which He created according to His will. May He establish His kingdom during your life and your days and during the life of all the house of Israel speedily and soon, and say: Amen.*

The assembly would then respond, *Amen. May His great name be blessed now and forever.*

That was the original Kaddish of antiquity. Later, in the medieval academies of Babylonia, the following paragraphs were added:

> *Blessed, praised and glorified, exalted, extolled and honored, magnified and lauded be the name of the Holy One, blessed be He, though He be high above all the blessings and hymns, praises and consolations, which are uttered in the world. And say: Amen.*
>
> *May the prayers and supplications of all Israel be acceptable to their Father who is in heaven, and say: Amen. May there be abundant peace from heaven and life for us and all Israel. And say: Amen.*

Almost all the above is in the Aramaic language, the language of the early rabbinic academies in both Jerusalem and Babylonia. Considerably later, a final verse was added, a pure Hebrew restatement of the last paragraph above. It is based on a verse in the book of Job (25:2):

> *May He who establishes peace in His heights establish peace for us and all Israel, And say: Amen.*

It should be noted that several modern prayer books used in liberal congregations add the words *"and all the inhabitants of the world"* before the final amen. And it should be noted also that there are other versions of the Kaddish that are not designated for recitation by mourners. The mourner's Kaddish is referred to as *Kaddish Yatom* (orphan's Kaddish). Then there is the *Hatzi Kaddish* (half Kaddish), which is chanted by the prayer leader in the synagogue to separate parts of the service; there is the *Kaddish Shalem* (complete Kaddish) recited by the prayer leader before the conclusion of the service, which adds a verse asking that the prayers that have been offered be accepted by God; and there is the *Kaddish D'Rabbanan* (rabbinic Kaddish), which is recited after reading passages from the writings of the early rabbis.

There is actually one other version of the Kaddish that *does* make reference to death. It is prescribed for recitation by the children of the deceased at the conclusion of the funeral service at the graveside, and it is the only version of the Kaddish that makes mention of death. It is called *Kaddish D'ithadeta,* derived from words added to the first sentence the first paragraph: *"Di hu atid l'ithadeta . . . in the world that is to be created anew, when He will revive the dead and raise them up to eternal life."* This is a late medieval addition to the Kaddish that otherwise makes no reference to death. As we have said, Kaddish is a doxology, a hymn of praise to God, very much like the well-known Christian doxology, "The Lord's Prayer" (Matt. 6:9–13 et seq.). Like all scholars of Jerusalem in his day, Jesus was certainly familiar with the Kaddish and very likely paraphrased it for his followers with the instruction: *"This is how you should pray."*

Now that we are familiar with the text and origins of the Kaddish, it remains to be asked, should a person who does not believe in a place of reward and punishment after death—a person who recognizes that all the millions of words that have been spoken and written to describe the torments of hell and the euphoria of heaven are speculative inventions at best—should such a person recite the Kaddish after the death of a loved one?

I find the answer to that question in the very first sentence of the Kaddish:

> *B'alma di v'ra khirutai*—in the world which was created by the will of God.

If we believe that God, the Infinite Intelligence, is the creator of the world and of humanity; that it is God who inspired the evolutionary process that gave birth to our parents, to our families, and to ourselves "by the will of God"; and if we are appreciative of our own place in this process, then it would seem natural to feel an upwelling of gratitude from time to time, especially at moments of deep emotion and yearning. I am grateful beyond words for gifts that I received from my parents, grandparents, and friends. There are not adequate words in my vocabulary, and so when I think of them, I turn to sacred tradition and humbly recite, *Yitgadal ve-yitkadash shemei rabbah.*

We have spoken about the nature of God, about the efficacy of prayer, about the role of the individual in God's world, and about death and its aftermath, and we have attempted to convey a concept of God devoid of anthropomorphism, superstition, and pious cant. So in the words of Ecclesiastes,

> *The sum of the matter, when all is said and done.*

What is the sum of the matter? What have we learned about God and about our place in God's universe after billions of years of physical and intellectual evolution? Ecclesiastes summed it all up with the admonition: *"Revere God and observe God's commandments"* (12:13). I cannot improve on that formula, except to add the caveat that we not think of God and the commandments the way that the author of Ecclesiastes and his generation very likely did. The God for grown-ups created a world of inexorable law, and so the task of the human being is to study that law, to delve deeply into the nature of the universe so that we may come closer to the quests of Moses and Albert Einstein: to "know" God. And what of the commandments? the mitzvot? We must follow the lead of Martin Buber and examine each and every one of them and decide, based on our study and our love for humanity, which of them are "of God" and which derive from a primitive concept of God that demeans God and that fosters the superstitions that many accept today as religion.

"When all is said and done," I recommend to my readers a prayer that I love and that was recited with love by Jews since the first century:

> *Ilu finu malei shira ka-yam—*
> *Were our mouths filled with song as water fills the sea,*
> *and our lips rang with Your praise as tirelessly as the roaring waves;*
> *If our lips offered adoration as boundless as the sky,*
> *and our eyes shone in reverence as brightly as the sun;*
> *If our hands were spread in prayer as wide as eagles wings,*
> *and our feet ran to serve You as swiftly as the deer;*
> *We would still be unable to thank You adequately*
> *for the smallest fraction of the numberless bounties*
> *that You bestowed on our ancestors and upon us.*
> (As translated in Siddur Hadash, p. 215)

What numberless bounties? The authors of this prayer continued by specifying the gifts that they had in mind: redemption from Egyptian bondage, sustaining our ancestors in times of famine, and the like. (In the Passover Haggadah, there is a long list of these gifts that the rabbis credited to God: again, redemption from Egyptian bondage and the splitting of the Red Sea, the giving of the Torah, the Sabbath, manna in the wilderness, etc.) All these gifts are sung out in joy, each followed by the lusty refrain *Dayenu—It would have been enough for us.*

But what does this phrase *"the numberless bounties"* mean to the person who does not believe that the Infinite Intelligence that we call God interferes in the process of human history? To the person who does not believe that God split the sea or thundered the commandments from Mount Sinai? Why do I love that ancient prayer and delight in thanking God for numberless bounties? (Actually, the word *numberless* is a pale translation of the original Hebrew *"al ahat me-alef elef alfai alafim ve-ribai revavot*"—for even one of the thousands upon tens of thousands multiplied again and again.)

I love the fact that God created those aquatic creatures who emerged from the seas billions of years ago with incipient capacities for love, for intellectual pursuit, for the appreciation of aesthetics, for empathy, for the retention of the accumulated wisdom of former generations, for pleasure, and for so much more of what enables us to search, along with Moses and Einstein, for the meaning of God. These are the numberless bounties that the Infinite Intelligence that we call God has bestowed upon us. And so I have no hesitation in proclaiming my love for God, as did my grandfather. He praised the God of Abraham, Isaac, and Jacob, the God who thundered at Sinai; I praise the God of Infinite Intelligence who created us with the gift/curse of free will. That is the sum of the matter, when all is said and done.

There is paean of gratitude to God, similar to the *Ilu finu* above, that was restated poetically in a medieval prayer, *Akdamut*, which is chanted by congregations on the festival of *Shavuot* before the reading of the Torah, I offer it as a fitting conclusion to our search:

> *Could we with ink the ocean fill,*
> *Were every blade of grass a quill,*
> *Were the world of parchment made,*
> *And everyone a scribe by trade ---*
> *To write the love of God above*
> *Would drain the ocean dry;*
> *Nor would that scroll contain the whole*
> *Though stretched from sky to sky.* (As translated in *Daily Prayer Book*, Hertz, p. 419)

Our task as mature and rational human beings is to search for the meaning and dimensions of God's universe. If that search includes moments of prayer, the purpose of each prayer should be to bring us just one step closer to an understanding of what God wants of us. We begin with Micah's formulation. *What does Adonai require of you? To do justice, to love kindness, and to walk humbly with God* (6:8). And then we proceed to the sacred task of approaching the edges of divinity, knowing full well that neither we, nor our children, nor our children's children will ever comprehend the Infinite Intelligence that is God.

There is no better way to conclude our search for an adult understanding of God than to restate the timeless aphorism of Rabbi Tarfon:

> *You are not expected to complete the task, but you are not free to slough it off.*

Addendum

Two Timely Sermons: "*Truth*" and "*Amos 5779*"
and
Adonai over the Mighty Waters

Sermons delivered at Bowdoin College and a *D'var Torah*

Truth

Rosh Ha-Shanah Morning, 5778
Bowdoin College September 21, 2017

On this sacred day, a day when we should be moved to rededicate ourselves to the ideals of our faith, I want to discuss one of Judaism's most basic ideals, an ideal which is under severe assault today but that should be the basis for all human interaction. It is an ideal that we are instructed by our tradition to live by if we believe in *tikkun olam*—partnership with God in the sacred task of repairing our world. That ideal, dear friends, is Truth.

Our Jewish tradition teaches us over and over again that to serve God is to seek truth. One of the great sages of the Talmud, Rabbi Hanina, taught that the way that we come to recognize God is through truth. He taught: "*Hotamo shel ha-Kadosh baruch hu emet*—The seal of God is truth" (Talmud, Tractate Shabbat 55a and Yoma 69b). In other words, the way we recognize what is godly is to ask, Is it true?

Is it true?

We have heard over and over again from the highest sources that Latinos and Muslims should be barred from our country, that they should be rooted out and deported, even those who were brought here as children—the "dreamers"—because they are criminals and rapists. Let's go to every college in the country, including Bowdoin, to find where those "dreamers" might be hiding and send them back to a country that they never knew. And let's spend billions to build a wall to keep them out!

Should we listen to those rantings passively or should we demand truth? After all, we're not Muslims or Latinos. Why should it matter to us? But our Torah teaches us that we should treat the stranger as the homeborn. Further, our Torah teaches us that we should not stand idly by when we see injustice perpetrated against fellow human beings. If to believe in God requires us to seek truth, what should be our response to these ceaseless barrages of falsehoods against decent human beings? Our response, the response that teaches the godly ideal of truth is inscribed on the base of the Statue of Liberty: "Give me your tired, your poor, your huddled masses yearning to breathe free. Send these, the homeless, to me." *That* is truth.

We have been assured, again from the highest sources, that global warming is a hoax. With our own eyes, we see ice shelves in the Arctic split off, raising the levels of the oceans. With our own eyes, we see devastating weather patterns. With our own eyes, we see ocean water seeping up through the ground in areas of Florida. With our own eyes, we see choking smog in cities all over the world. The response? Our great nation withdraws from the Paris Climate Accords, because global warming is a hoax, and the reports of eye witnesses are fake news. But we read in the Psalms: "*Ha-aretz natan livnei adam*—God gave the earth to humankind." This earth was given to human beings in sacred trust. We are supposed to take care of it. *That* is truth.

Just a month ago, armed white men marched with Nazi banners and white supremacist regalia in Charlottesville, terrorizing a synagogue and plowing an automobile into a crowd killing an innocent woman. They marched with flaming torches chanting "Jews will not replace us! Jews will not replace us!" What message did we then receive from the leader of the free world? We were informed that there were good people on both sides. The hate mongers were equated with the decent people who were there to represent humanity and love. What does our tradition say about this? It's there in the book of Leviticus: "Love your neighbor as yourself." *That* is truth.

When you come into a synagogue, you should expect to learn something. So let's pause here for a little Hebrew lesson. Does anyone know the Hebrew word for truth? . . . Right; *emet*. That word *emet* occurs 127 times in our Bible and countless more times in the writings of the rabbis. As I said before, truth has always been a basic ideal in Judaism; it is through truth that we find God. So let's take a look at that word that means truth, *emet*.

Emet is made up of three Hebrew letters: *alef*, *mem* and *tav*. *Alef* is the first letter of the Hebrew alphabet; *mem* is a middle letter; and *tav* is the final letter. The beginning, the middle and the end; that is truth: the be all and the end all, the alpha and omega. In the *Unetaneh Tokef* prayer that we recited earlier in our service, the text refers to God metaphorically as sitting on the throne of *emet*—of truth. And then it goes on to say "*Emet ki ata hu dayan*—You are the One who judges by the standard of truth."

I mentioned a moment ago that the word *emet* occurs 127 times in the Bible. Let me give you just a few examples:

Jeremiah 10: *The Lord God is truth.*
Psalm 119: *Truth is the essence of [God's] word.*
Psalm 117: *The truth of God endures forever.*
Zechariah 8: *Love truth and peace.*

I could go on and on, but you get the idea. There is no other value in our Jewish tradition that is as venerated as *emet*—as truth.

Just incidentally, as I was thinking about this morning's message a few weeks ago, it occurred to me that the idealization of truth is not limited to the Bible and to our Jewish tradition. I attended a university whose motto is *Veritas*—truth. Our rabbinic student, Rachael Pass and our Hillel advisor, Rachel Connelly, are both graduates of Brandeis University. And what is the motto of Brandeis? *Emet*. Curiosity moved me to look up the mottoes of several other American universities, and I discovered that many of them chose either truth or veritas to characterize their educational goals. Johns Hopkins, Yale, Colgate, Northwestern, Pitt and many others – all of them project truth as the goal of education.

Now some of you might be wondering at this point: is that all that the rabbi has to tell us this Rosh Ha-Shanah morning? That truth is important? Haven't we known that ever since our parents taught us not to lie? What's new about truth this year?

Here we come to the crux of my message: What is new about truth this year? What's new is that truth is under assault here in America in ways as insidious as back in the 1930s in Germany. Back then we were taught about the danger of the big lie, that if someone in a position of power repeated a lie over and over again, it would become truth to those masses of people who are not equipped to differentiate between fact and fake. The Nazi propaganda machine was able to convince ordinary Germans through distortions of truth that Jews were inferior people, not worthy of life. Should we not be concerned when one of America's most reliable newspapers informs us that by careful count our President has uttered well over six thousand lies since his inauguration?

Just think back to those years during the Obama administration when accusation after accusation was hurled at the president that he was not a native born citizen of the United States. The purveyors of that big lie were called "birthers," and millions of people, full of resentments for all kinds of reasons, believed them and took as their hero the person who purveyed that big lie most loudly.

I can't characterize that technique of the big lie any better than the prophet Isaiah, who cried out:

> *Woe, to those who call evil good and good evil; who present darkness as light and light as darkness; who present bitter as sweet and sweet as bitter!* (Isa. 5:20)

And so what is my message to this Bowdoin congregation on the first day of the new year? Be alert; be discriminating as you read and listen to the news. The fact that something is repeated over and over again does not make it true. Do not think of truth as a simple cliché, as a value to be taken for granted. The future of this great country of ours depends on those who can separate truth from fiction and who have the courage to stand up and demand truth from the powerful.

It is said that "The only thing necessary for the triumph of evil is for good people to do nothing" (Attributed incorrectly to Edmund

Burke). To do nothing is to allow truth to be cast into the abyss. To do something, to expose falsehood and demand truth, is to honor God whose seal is Truth.

I turn to the words of the Psalmist to conclude this Rosh Ha-Shanah message:

> *Hesed v'emet nifgashu*—Faithfulness and truth meet; justice and well-being kiss. Truth springs up from the earth . . . (Ps. 85:11—2)

> *V'chen yehi ratzon*—May this be the will of God.

Amos, 5779

Yom Kippur Morning, 5779
Bowdoin College
September 19, 2018

I want to introduce you this Yom Kippur morning to one of the great heroes of Judaism, a man who should be well known but whose memory languishes in the Bible among those twelve whom we refer to as "The Minor Prophets." There are gems of wisdom in the writings of those so-called minor prophets. One of them, Micah, was the teacher who said: *"What does Adonai require of you? Only to do justice, to love goodness, and to walk modestly with God."* Another of those so-called minor prophets was Zechariah who quoted God as declaring: *"Not by might, nor by power, but by My spirit."* And there was Malachi who asked: *"Have we not all one father? Has not one God created us?"*

I could go on and on with magnificent utterances from that group of Israelite preachers whom we call "The Minor Prophets." Why were they labeled as "Minor?" Certainly not because their teachings were less important than others in the Bible. No, it is simply because their recorded prophecies were brief. Those who were labeled by our tradition as *Major* Prophets—Isaiah, Jeremiah, and Ezekiel—left us books of from 48 to 60 chapters, while the *Minor* Prophets each left us from one to fourteen chapters.

The man to whom I want to introduce you this morning was one of those minor prophets; he left us only nine chapters, and most Bible scholars believe that some of those chapters might have come from the pens of later editors. But let me begin by telling you why I think that Amos was one of our great heroes.

We don't know much about Amos, but we do know that he was a simple farmer. He described himself as a sheep breeder and a tender of sycamore trees. He denied that he was a professional prophet but said that he felt compelled to speak out. He heard God telling him to go and confront the king and the high priest, and so he left his farm and went. As he put it: *"If a lion roars, who can but fear; when God speaks, who can but prophesy."*

Just a bit of ancient history before I get to the heroism of Amos. After the glorious reigns of King David and King Solomon, the kingdom of Israel went through a civil war. As in the American Civil War, the north and south fought a bloody war and then split into two kingdoms; the northern kingdom was called Israel and the southern kingdom was called Judah. Jerusalem remained as the capital of Judah, and, at the time that Amos lived—in the eighth pre-Christian century—Bethel was the capital of Israel. Israel, the northern kingdom, was ruled by King Jeroboam and his chief advisor was the head priest of the shrine at Bethel, Amaziah. Together, Jeroboam and Amaziah ruled during a very prosperous period, but, as is so often the case during periods of prosperity, it was only the wealthy and powerful who prospered while the masses suffered degradation and poverty.

So Amos, the simple farmer, left his home in Judah and traveled northward to Bethel in Israel, hostile territory, to confront the people whom he saw as corrupting God's Torah. Now, you understand—Amos was a suspect alien in Bethel. He came from the land of Judah which had recently been at war with Israel. How was he, a stranger, going to get people to listen to his message? Well, he devised a clever stratagem. He went to the main square in Bethel, in front of the shrine of Amaziah the priest, near the palace of King Jeroboam. He knew that if he began his message with an attack on the leaders and the powerful of Israel, they wouldn't listen to him. They would probably pelt him with rotten fruit and yell, "Fake news! Fake news!"

What did he do? He got up on the steps of the shrine, and he began crying out against the enemies of Israel. First, he attacked Damascus for their treacherous attack on Israel from the north. Then he denounced the Philistines for plotting with the enemies of Israel. Then he attacked Tyre and Edom and Ammon and Moab for all kinds of bestial cruelties. And, as he attacked these mortal enemies of Israel, one after another, you can imagine how the crowd grew in that central square of Bethel. They must have been yelling "Right on! Give it to 'em! Go Amos!"

And then this man from Judah delivered a strong attack against his own land! He accused the Judeans of spurning the Torah and practicing idolatry. Israel had just fought a war against Judah, and so the crowd was now a frenzied mob. They loved everything that Amos was preaching. "More! More!" I can hear them shouting. "Go Amos!!" He had them where he wanted them, listening with glee to every word from his mouth, and then—I can see him raising his hands to quiet the mob, and then.

Then Amos delivered the blistering message that he had come to deliver. I'll quote now from the actual text:

Thus said Adonai: I will not revoke my decree against Israel because they have sold for silver those whose cause was just; they have sold the needy for a pair of sandals. Ah, you who trample the heads of the poor into the dust of the ground, and push the humble out of your way. Father and son go together to the same girl and profane My holy name. . . .

There was a lot more condemnation of the immorality of especially the wealthy and powerful of Israel, and then Amos went on, again speaking for God:

I will punish Israel for its transgression; I will wreak judgment on the altar of Bethel . . . I will wreck the winter palace together with the summer palace . . . and the great houses shall be destroyed.

As you can imagine, the crowd was now aghast. Here was this stranger speaking out against them and even against the king and the high priest. Some of them went running to Amaziah in the shrine to let him know that an alien was denouncing them in the main square.

Immediately Amaziah sent a message to King Jeroboam to let him know that Amos was conspiring against his kingdom. Quote: *"The country cannot endure the things he is saying."*

And then Amaziah went outside to confront this rabble-rouser. He went up to Amos and said, in the name of King Jeroboam: *"Seer, off with you to the land of Judah. . . Don't ever prophesy again at Bethel, for it is a king's sanctuary and a royal palace."* "Off with you to the land of Judah!" Jeroboam didn't like aliens from the south.

Needless to say, Amos did not back down. He answered that he was not a prophet, and that he had no choice but to deliver the message that God had given him. He said a few words about the punishment that awaited King Jeroboam and Amaziah, and then he turned back to the crowd and delivered the ultimate insult:

To Me, O Israelites, declares God, you are just like the Ethiopians.

Let me explain: Here in the United States, we've heard a lot lately about what is called "the N word." Well, in ancient Israel, Ethiopian was "the N word." It means the lowliest of people, the ones to whom you feel superior. It would be as if someone were to confront our president and vice-president and the leaders of the Senate and the House and say to them: "In the eyes of God, you are not any better than those Hispanic mothers whose children you ripped from their bosoms and then stuck in cages. You are no better than the African Americans whom you barred from voting in Alabama because they did not have drivers' licenses."

To Me, O Israelites, you are just like the Ethiopians. . . .

In the eyes of God, every human being is equal, Israelites like Ethiopians.

I cannot leave Amos without one final quotation from this so-called minor prophet. Remember, he was delivering his message on the steps of the shrine in Bethel where the priests and the wealthy people, after victimizing the poor, gathered piously to offer sacrifices and sing hymns to God. This is one of my favorite passages in the Bible. Speaking for God, Amos cries out:

I loathe, I hate your festivals. . . . When you offer Me your sacrifices, I will not accept them. . . . Spare me the sound of your hymns, and let Me not hear the music of your lutes, But let justice well up like waters and righteousness like a mighty stream.

O Amos, how we need you today here in America! *Let justice well up like waters and righteousness as a mighty stream!*

Friends, let's take a flight of imagination. Amos is reincarnated. He walks through the streets of America observing and listening. If you are familiar with Alexis de Tocqueville's masterful book *Democracy in America*, written in 1831, you will remember that that is exactly what de Tocqueville did. Sponsored by the government of France, he traveled all over the young American democracy taking notes on everything that he saw. Everywhere he went, he listened and he observed, and then he wrote his masterpiece. And so that is what I would have our reincarnated Amos do today—listen and observe.

As he wanders through America, he hears the scientists warning of climate change and the rising of the oceans as the polar ice caps melt and the hurricanes intensify. But no; King Jeroboam says that climate change is a hoax. He hears about Sandy Hook and the Las Vegas massacre and Parkland High School and, because he is sane, he realizes that there must be controls on the availability of guns. But no; Jeroboam depends upon the support of the National Rifle Association. He reads the inscription on the Statue of Liberty inviting the "huddled masses yearning to breathe free" to come to the land of the free to become part of the American dream, and he hears Jeroboam crying "Off with you, Mexican rapists, to the land that you came from!"

He hears that, in the land of liberty and justice for all, neo-Nazis are marching, threatening and shouting anti-Black and anti-Semitic slogans. But Jeroboam says that there are good people on both sides. He hears that a powerful foreign country has annexed the land of another nation and is threatening the security of its neighbors, but Jeroboam admires the despotic leader of that country and denigrates the leaders of friendly democracies. Our reincarnated Amos sees the lack of nutrition and medical care for the needy in the wealthiest country in the world and wonders at the amount of time that Jeroboam spends in his winter and summer palaces, Mar a Lago and Bedminster, thinking about spending billions to erect a wall to keep out . . . Ethiopians. Amos has known from childhood that God intends for us to respect and love our neighbors, but the example set by King Jeroboam is one of nastiness, indecency, the abuse of women, and the perversion of truth. And when called to task by a free press, he cries: "Fake news!"

And so Amos goes to Bethel—let's make that Washington—and he climbs up the steps of the Capitol and he cries out: *"You have sold for silver those whose cause was just, . . . You who trample the heads of the poor into the dust of the ground . . . Let justice well up like waters and righteousness like a mighty stream."*

How sorely we need a prophet today to confront power and indecency with moral courage the way that Amos confronted King Jeroboam and Amaziah in the name of God. We may not be prophets, but we are the descendants of prophets, and it is our task as Jews to devote our lives to truth and to *tikkun olam*—the improvement of our imperfect world. It is our task to work for that day when *"justice will well up as waters and righteousness like a mighty stream."*

When we hear that final shofar blast at the conclusion of our Yom Kippur services, may it awaken us to act as the daughters and sons of prophets like Amos, condemning the lies, the bullying, the greed, the immorality and the abuses of power that today characterize our nation's leadership.

The Torah teaches us: "*Tzedek tzedek tirdof*—Justice justice shall you pursue." It is our sacred task to add our voices and our strength and our votes to those who have the courage and the decency to work for a more just and equitable society for all the children of God.

Adonai over the Mighty Waters

It was during my early childhood that I was introduced to the Psalms as something more than chanted bits of liturgy. I was seven years old when my parents took me to see my first movie, *Captains Courageous*, starring Spencer Tracy and Freddie Bartholomew. The story tells of the bravery of the sea captains and crews who sailed out of Gloucester Harbor in the days of the clipper ships. A few weeks after we saw the movie, we went on a family excursion to Gloucester (only about forty miles from our seaside home in Winthrop), and there my father pointed out the monument that memorializes those generations of intrepid Gloucester seafarers who made the town famous.

Inscribed on the base of that monument were the words *"They who go down to the sea in ships."* As we stood there viewing it, my father, ever the Hebrew pedagogue, recited three words: *Yordei ha-yam ba-oniyot*. I asked him what those words meant, and he answered that it was the original Hebrew of the inscription on the monument, that it came from *Tehillim*, and that he would show it to me when we got home.

Back home, my father took out his Hebrew-English Bible and had me read verses 23–30 of Psalm 107 aloud, both in Hebrew and English.

> *They who go down to the sea in ships, who ply their trade in the mighty waters, they have seen the works of Adonai and His wonders in the deep. By His word He raised a storm wind that made the waves surge. Mounting up to the heaven, plunging down to the depths, disgorging in their misery. They reeled and*

staggered like a drunken man, all their skill to no avail. In their adversity they cried to Adonai, and He saved them from their troubles. He reduced the storm to a whisper; the waves were stilled.

I may have been only seven years old, but that dramatic description of the turbulent sea and of God's power over it was etched into my memory, not only because of the Gloucester monument and the movie, but because it was during that same year that my father, who loved a day of fishing in a small dory a mile or two out in the Atlantic from Winthrop Beach, took me along for the first time. On that occasion and on the dozens that followed with my father and me in a small dory, I learned to respect those ocean swells—*mounting up, plunging down.*

In the spring: my visit to Gloucester; in the summer: my first ocean adventure, and then in the fall—

Our home was situated less than a hundred yards from the ocean, and each night the sound of the sea gently lapping at the rocky shore lulled me to sleep. I awoke on Wednesday morning, September 21, 1938, to the good news that school was cancelled that day because of the hurricane that was streaking toward Boston. My parents kept the radio on through breakfast, and we heard about unparalleled devastation on Long Island caused by, as one announcer christened it, "the Yankee Clipper," and another, "the Long Island Express." And it was headed our way.

By the time we finished breakfast, we could see the branches of the trees alongside our house whipping around menacingly and the trees themselves arching northward. Then came the rains in piercing sheets, drumming on the windows and even penetrating a few. My father wanted to feel for himself the fury of nature by going down to the shore drive, and I, ignoring my mother's warnings, insisted on accompanying him.

We fought the wind as we traversed the short distance from our house to the seawall, I holding tightly to my father's hand. We had to shout to be heard over the gale and the roaring of the violent sea. Within moments of our arrival, the seawall at the next corner crumbled, leaving a gaping and widening chasm in the middle of the shore drive. Inevitably, as we watched in disbelief, the front of the venerable Victorian Sea Breeze Hotel slid into the chasm. By this time, we were soaked by the swirling spume of both the driving rain and the crashing waves. And then, when a utility pole crashed down not ten feet from us and the wires started whipping around, my father decided that it was time to beat a retreat. But before we left, my father cried out, as if challenging the sea:

Mi-kolot mayim rabim adirim mishb'rai yam, adir ba-marom Adonai!

I hadn't recognized the verse that my father uttered at the Gloucester monument, but I recognized this one from the *Kabbalat Shabbat* service that I attended each week, standing at my father's side. I had no idea what it meant or why my father chose to exclaim it at such a stunning moment, but as soon as we got home, he, ever the pedagogue, again took out his Bible and had me read the verses of Psalm 93 in Hebrew and English. And as I did so, I somehow connected the idea of God's power over *"the thunder of the mighty waters, more majestic than the breakers of the sea"* with *"the storm wind that made the waves surge"* of Psalm 107. And I loved the sound of those Hebrew words, as my father intoned them onomatopoeically—*mishb'rai yam*, breakers of the sea—those titanic waves that washed over us as we stood transfixed by the power of the hurricane.

It is now almost fourscore years since my dramatic introductions to Psalms 107 and 93, but lurking in the back of my mind over the years has been the notion that our lyrical ancestors were fascinated by the power of God over the elements, particularly over the waters and even more particularly over *tehom(ot)*—usually translated as the watery depths. The word *tehom* in its various forms occurs thirty-six times in the Bible. We are first introduced to *tehom* in the second verse of the Torah as God, about to initiate the creative process, confronts the darkness over the surface of *tehom*. God defeats the darkness by creating light on the first day and establishes mastery over the inchoate watery depths on the second day by separating *"water from water."*

I am not qualified to delve into the origins of the word *tehom* other than to say that many Bible scholars suggest that *tehom* is derived from a Mesopotamian creation story, which tells that the earth was formed from the carcass of the sea dragon, Tiamat. I do not think that it is unreasonable, though, to come to the conclusion that those thirty-six appearances of *tehom* in biblical texts, most of which tell of Adonai's dominance over *tehom,* hark back to those ancient creation stories. As, for example, in the story of Noah: God brings on the flood by bursting the fountains of *tehom* and ends the flood by stopping up the fountains of *tehom* (Gen. 7:11, 8:2).

There are many examples of God's mastery over *tehom* in the Bible, but it is to Psalms that I want to return with a series of examples of the awe of the authors over the power of God as illustrated by God's control over not only *tehom* but over all the elements of nature: the waters, the rivers, the oceans, the rains, the seas—all the tributaries of *tehom.* At the time that most of the Psalms were composed, the various nations around the eastern Mediterranean had pantheons that included gods who were supposed to regulate those natural phenomena. And so it is not difficult to understand why the various psalmists, writing over half a millennium, again and again sang praises to the God whom they revered as the master not only of *tehom* but of all the forces of nature.

I invite the reader to share my wonder at the majesty of these verses:

> *Adonai over the mighty waters. . . Adonai sat enthroned over the flood.* (29:3, 10)

> *The ocean bed was exposed; the foundations of the world were laid bare by Your mighty roaring, Adonai.* (Ps. 18:16)

> *He heaps up the ocean waters like a mound, stores **tehomot** in vaults.* (33:7)

> *Where **tehom** calls to **tehom** in the roar of Your cataracts; all Your breakers and billows have swept over me.* (42:8)

Who by His powers fixed the mountains firmly, who is girded with might, who stills the raging seas, the raging waves. (65:8)

It was You who drove back the sea with Your might, who smashed the heads of the monsters in the waters, . . . It was You who released the springs and torrents, who made the rivers run dry. (74:13–15)

The waters saw You, O God, the waters saw You and were convulsed; the **tehomot** *quaked as well, Clouds streamed water, . . . Your way was through the sea, Your path through the mighty waters.* (77:17–20)

You rule the swelling of the sea; when its waves stir, You still them. (89:10)

The ocean sounds, Adonai, the ocean sounds its thunder, the ocean sounds its pounding. Above the thunder of the mighty waters, more majestic than the breakers of the sea is Adonai, majestic on high. (93:3–4)

Let the sea and all within it thunder, the world and its inhabitants; let the rivers clap their hands, the mountains sing joyously together at the presence of Adonai. (98:7–9)

You made **tehom** *cover it as a garment; The waters stood above the mountains. They fled at Your blast, rushed away at the sound of Your thunder . . . You make springs gush forth in torrents.* (104:6–10)

Whatever Adonai desires He does in heaven and earth, in the seas and all the **tehomot.** (135:6)

Praise Adonai, O you who are on earth, all sea monsters and **tehomot** *. . . storm wind that executes His command.* (148:7–8)

I want to add to these excerpts from Psalms just a few more biblical citations that amplify the awe of the psalmists at the power of God over the mighty waters. There are paeans to Wisdom in both the books of Proverbs and Job, and in both of those hymns, there are homages to God's power over *tehom*, over the mighty waters:

> [Wisdom speaks:] *There was still no **tehom** when I was brought forth, no springs rich in water; . . . I was there . . . when He set the heaven above firm, and the fountains of **tehom** gushed forth; when He assigned the sea its limits, so that its waters never transgress His command.* (Proverbs 8:24, 27–29)

> *For He sees to the ends of the earth, observes all that is beneath the heavens; when He fixed the weight of the winds, set the measure of the waters; when He made a rule for the rain and a course for the thunderstorms. Then He saw it and gauged it; He measured it and probed it.* (Job 28:24–27)

Having now made reference to the book of Job, I cannot resist concluding this essay on the power of God over the mighty waters with one final citation that inspires wonder every time I confront it. From the peerless chapter 38, beginning with stupefying challenge: *Where were you when I laid the earth's foundations?*

> *Who closed the sea behind doors when it gushed forth out of the womb, when I clothed it in clouds, swaddled it in dense clouds, When I made breakers My limits for it, and set up its bar and doors, and said: "You may come so far and no farther, here your surging waves will stop." . . . Have you penetrated the sources of the sea, or walked in the recesses of **tehom**?* (38:8–11)

Ever the rationalist, yet I respond viscerally to the images of God overwhelming *tehom*, of God enthroned above the mighty waters, of God who stills the raging seas. Do I understand? No, . . . yet I join Moses and Miriam who sang at the shore of the sea: *Zeh Eili—This is my God!*

Acknowledgements

I owe profound debts of gratitude to many, but I will begin with my rabbis -- some were learned teachers, some were exemplars of Jewish leadership, some were both, and all of them served and loved the Jewish People. I list them here with admiration and with a heart-felt *Kaddish*:

Rabbi Maurice Zigmond, Rabbi Theodore Gordon, Rabbi Sheldon Blank, Rabbi Jacob R. Marcus, Rabbi Mordecai Kaplan, Rabbi Ira Eisenstein, Rabbi Jacob J. Weinstein, Rabbi David Polish, Rabbi Roland Gittelsohn, Rabbi Gunther Plaut, and Rabbi Jack Stern.

There were others, but these in particular were my distinguished and beloved mentors. I must add two more of my mentors, not rabbis, to this list: Elie Wiesel and, still among the living, Amos Oz.

My first teacher, he who taught me to love the cadences of prayer and the magnificence of the Bible and Jewish literature, was *avi mori,* my father and teacher, *Hazzan* Leon Masovetsky. He would have disagreed with much that is in this book, but he would have enjoyed reading it and recommending it to friends. He had a wonderful tenor voice, and I included the folksong, *A Dudele,* in the first chapter not only to make a point but also because I can still hear his poignant rendition of it.

Much of this book was inspired by the thinking of Albert Einstein, and I am grateful to the Albert Einstein Archives at Hebrew University for permission to use the Einstein quotations. It is worth mentioning that, a few decades before my tenure as Senior Rabbi of Congregation Keneseth Israel of Elkins Park, Einstein spoke at K.I. and accepted an honorary membership.

And finally, my dear wife for sixty-five blessed years, Judith Blumberg Maslin. She has truly been my *ezer k'negdo,* my helpmate and partner. Together we served our congregations and raised our beloved family. That family now includes two bright great-grandsons, Daniel and Yitzhak, who, I pray, will achieve the wisdom and the strength to continue the life-long search for a God for grown-ups.

Index

A

"A Dudele," 10
Abraham, x, 1, 3, 9–11, 21, 30–31, 75, 84
Abraham Ibn Ezra, 47
Adam and Eve, 6
Adonai, v, 16–19, 28–29, 31, 33, 36–39, 41–44, 48–50, 53, 55, 71, 85, 87, 100–101, 103–4
Akeidah, 30–31
Alabama, 97
Aleinu, 57
Alighieri, Dante, 76
Allah, 21, 76
Amalek, 34
Amaziah, 95–97, 99
Amos, 29–30, 33, 39–40, 95–99
Aquinas, Thomas, 76
Aramaic, 79–80
Archimedes, 39
Atlantic, 101
Augustine (saint), 39
Auschwitz, 2, 16, 51, 58, 62
Avinu Malkeinu, x
Avodah Zarah, 67

Aztecs, 70

B

Babylonian, 27, 37, 62, 69, 72–73
Bartholomew, Freddie, 100
Bava Metzia, 25
Beatrice, 76
Bedminster, 98
Beethoven, Ludwig van, 64
Bethel, 95–97, 99
Bible, v, x, 1, 11, 21–23, 25–27, 30–32, 34–36, 38–40, 42–44, 46, 71, 91, 94, 102–3
Boaz, 40
Bowdoin, 87, 89, 92, 94
Bowie, Walter Russel, 69, 78
B'rit, 54
Brothers Karamazov, The (Dostoyevsky), 13
Buber, Martin, 9, 34, 46, 56, 83
Buddha, 39

C

Captains Courageous, 100

Cervantes, Miguel de, 39
Chanukah, 54
Charlottesville, 90
Christianity, 25, 36, 47, 49, 65–66, 70, 75
Confucius, 39
Conservative, 17
Copernicus, Nicolaus, 39
Cossacks, 62
Crusaders, 62

D

Damascus, 96
Daniel, 44
David (king), 95
Dayenu, 54, 83
Declaration of the Rights of Man, 30
Dei Verbum, 26
Demeter, 70
Deutero-Isaiah, 27, 37
Deuteronomy, 18, 26–27, 44, 46, 50, 55, 78
Dmitri (charater in *The Brothers Karamazov*), 13
Dostoyevsky, Fyodor
Brothers Karamazov, The, 13
D'var Torah, 87

E

Ecclesiastes, 38–39, 44, 82–83
Egypt, 28, 78
Eileh Ezkerah, 5–6
Einstein, Albert, 1, 4, 7–8, 15, 31, 35, 46, 56, 83
Elchanan, 64–65
Eliezer (rabbi), 24–25, 66

Elijah, 25, 59
emet, 77, 91
Ephraim, 42
Ethics (Baruch Spinoza), 5, 67
Ethiopian, 97–98
Evangelicals, 25, 49
Exodus, 26, 36, 50
Ezekiel, 26, 41–42, 44, 79, 94

F

Fertile Crescent, 27, 36
Forgotten, The (Elie Wiesel), 64
free will, 6–7, 59–60, 63, 84
Freud, 39

G

Gan Eden, 73
Gates of Prayer, 16
Gehinnom, 73–76, 79–80
Genesis, 6, 26–27, 38, 57
ger, 40
Gilgamesh, 27, 69, 72
Gittelsohn, Roland, 56
Gloucester, 100–102
goi kadosh, 51–52, 57
Golden Age, 8, 62

H

Hades, 70, 75
Haggadah, 78, 83
Hagigah, 49
Halakhah, 24–25
Haman, 59
Ha-motzi, 54

Hanina (rabbi), 89
Hassidim, 48
Hebrew, 11, 39, 84, 100, 102
hell, 65, 75–77
Hertz, 84
Heschel, Abraham, 20, 52
Hillel, 78, 91
Hitler, Adolf, 59, 62
Hiyya bar Abba (rabbi), 49
Holiness Code, 53
Holocaust, 2–3, 7, 58, 60, 62–64
Homer, 39
Hosea, 39, 42, 61
huppah, 54

I

Inferno, 76
Infinite Intelligence, 8–9, 12, 78, 82–85
infinity, 4–5, 7, 12, 39, 48, 79
Isaiah, x, 11–12, 22, 28, 33, 35, 39–41, 92, 94
Ishmael, 6
Ishmael (rabbi), 6
Ishtar, 69
Isis, 70
Islam, 36, 49, 65, 76
Israelite, 30–32, 34, 44, 94
Ivanov, Vyachislav, 22

J

Jacob (rabbi), 66, 71
Jahannam, 76
Jeremiah, 19, 22, 31, 39, 41–42, 49, 91, 94
Jeroboam, 95, 97–99

Jeroboam (king), 95, 97–99
Jesus, 22, 47, 66, 70, 81
Jewish, 5, 17–19, 47, 49–50, 52–54, 57, 72
Job, 1, 3–4, 38–39, 44, 46, 64, 72, 74, 80, 105
Joseph, 6, 23, 28
Joseph, Akiba ben, 23, 59, 74
Joshua (rabbi), 24–25, 35
Josiah (king), 30–31
Judah, 27, 30–31, 62, 95–97
Judaism, 1, 23, 25, 36, 47, 49–50, 52, 59, 66, 70, 74, 89, 91, 94
Jung, Carl, 70

K

Kabbalat Shabbat, 102
Kaddish, 16, 52, 74, 79–82
kadosh, 52–53, 89
Karaites, 23, 48
Kiddush, 52
Kiddushin, 52–53
Kierkegaard, 30
King Lear (Shakespeare), 64

L

Las Vegas, 98
Latinos, 89–90
Lazarus, 75
Leviticus, 31–32, 53, 90
Long Island, 101
Luke, 75–76

M

Maimonides, 1, 5, 9, 12, 22, 32, 35, 39, 47, 55–56, 66, 74

Sefer Ha-Mitzvot, 55
Makkot, 55
Malachi, 94
Mar a Lago, 98
Mark, 75
Marranos, 51
Matthew, 75
Megillah, 54
Menahot, 23
Messiah, 32
mezuzah, 54
Micah, 39, 85, 94
Michelangelo, x, 39, 64
midrash, 24–25, 73
mikdash me-at, 54
minor prophets, 94
Mishna Avot, 59, 66–67, 71
Mishnah Eduyot, 74
Mishna Peah, 19
Mishna Sanhedrin, 70
Mitnagdim, 48
mitzvah, 54, 56–57, 67
mitzvot, 54–57, 65, 67, 71, 83
Moabite, 40
Moloch, 30–31
Moses, 1, 8, 11–12, 21–24, 26–27, 32, 35–36, 46, 48, 56, 78–79, 83–84, 105
Mount Sinai, 25, 50, 84
Muhammed, 22
Muslims, 89–90
Mussaf, 17–18

N

Nahmanides, 47
Nathan (rabbi), 25
Nazi, 43, 58, 90, 92

New York Times, 51
Nicene Creed, 47
Night (Elie Wiesel), 62
Noah, 26, 44, 103
Numbers, 5, 27, 33, 56

O

Obama (administration), 92
Ophelia, 52
ordeal of jealousy, 56
Orthodox, 17, 22, 32, 49
Osiris, 70

P

Paradise, 76
Parkland, 98
Passover, 17, 54, 78, 83
Pater Noster, x
Pentateuch, 23, 32
Persephone, 70
Pharaoh, 59
Pharisees, 48, 66, 71, 75
Philistines, 96
Pogroms, 51
Polish, 62
prayer, 9, 13, 16–17, 20, 29, 81, 84
Price, Leontyne, 15
Proverbs, 44, 105
Psalmist, 1, 6, 13, 27, 93
Psalms, 38, 49, 53, 90, 102–3, 105
Purgatory, 76
Purim, 54

Q

Quetzalcoatl, 70
Quran, 21, 76–77

R

Rabad, 47
Rachel, 28, 41–42, 91
Reform, 56
Resurrection, 42, 66, 70–73
Reward and punishment, 65, 74, 76–77, 79, 81
Rite of Spring, 53
Romans, 5, 34, 62, 66, 71
Rosh HaShanah, 30, 73–74
Russian Pale, 51
Ruth, 39–40

S

Sabbath, 7, 17–18, 53–54, 83
Sadducees, 23, 48, 66, 71
Samuel, 34
Sandy Hook, 98
Saul (king), 34
Science, 1, 4
seder, 54
Sefer Ha-Mitzvot (Maimonides), 55
Shaharit, 18
Shakespeare, William, 39, 64, 72
King Lear, 64
Shammai (school), 73
Shema, 18–19, 37, 48, 51
siddur, 83
Simlai (rabbi), 55
Sinai, 11, 23, 25, 50, 78, 84
Socrates, 39
Solomon (king), 4, 95
Song of Songs, 38–39, 44

Sotah, 34
Spinoza, Baruch, 5, 48, 67
Ethics, 5, 67
Stern, Chaim, 16
Stravinsky, Igor, 53

T

Talmud, 34, 49, 55, 67, 73, 89
Tammuz, 69
Tarfon (rabbi), 67, 85
tehom, 102–5
Thirteen Principles of Faith, 74
Thomas, Dylan, 69
Tiamat, 103
Tocqueville, Alexis de, 98
Torah, 6, 8–9, 17, 19, 21–25, 27, 30–33, 39–40, 49–50, 55–56, 60, 70–71, 83–84, 90, 95–96
Torquemada, 59
Tracy, Spencer, 100
Treblinka, 58
truth, v, 1, 51, 77, 87, 89–93, 99

U

Unetaneh Tokef, 67, 91

V

Valley of Hinnom, 30, 73
Vatican, 26
Verga, Solomon ibn, 63
Vinci, Leonardo da, 39

W

Weatherhead, L. D., 13
Wiesel, Elie, 2, 62–64
Forgotten, The, 64
Night, 62
Winthrop, 100–101
Witt, Louis, 9

Y

Yankee Clipper, 101
Yehudah ha-Levi, 8

Yitzhak, Levi, 10
Yochanan ben Zakkai (rabbi), 34
Yom Kippur, 5, 16, 94, 99

Z

Zechariah, 94
Zeh Eili, 105
Zion, 28–29

Made in the USA
Middletown, DE
23 August 2019